Virgil Swift

God's Plan for His Chosen:
The Cost and the Conflict

Walt Thrun (signature)

WALT THRUN

WESTBOW
PRESS®
A DIVISION OF THOMAS NELSON
& ZONDERVAN

Scripture quotations taken from the New American Standard Bible®, Copyright © 1960, 1962, 1963, 1968, 1971, 1972, 1973, 1975, 1977, 1995 by The Lockman Foundation. Used by permission. (www.Lockman.org)

Scripture taken from the Holy Bible, NEW INTERNATIONAL VERSION®. Copyright © 1973, 1978, 1984, 2011 by Biblica, Inc. All rights reserved worldwide. Used by permission. NEW INTERNATIONAL VERSION® and NIV® are registered trademarks of Biblica, Inc. Use of either trademark for the offering of goods or services requires the prior written consent of Biblica US, Inc.

Scripture taken from the New King James Version. Copyright © 1979, 1980, 1982 by Thomas Nelson, Inc. Used by permission. All rights reserved.

WestBow Press books may be ordered through booksellers or by contacting:

WestBow Press
A Division of Thomas Nelson & Zondervan
1663 Liberty Drive
Bloomington, IN 47403
www.westbowpress.com
1 (866) 928-1240

Because of the dynamic nature of the Internet, any web addresses or links contained in this book may have changed since publication and may no longer be valid. The views expressed in this work are solely those of the author and do not necessarily reflect the views of the publisher, and the publisher hereby disclaims any responsibility for them.

Any people depicted in stock imagery provided by Thinkstock are models, and such images are being used for illustrative purposes only. Certain stock imagery © Thinkstock.

ISBN: 978-1-5127-2637-4 (sc)
ISBN: 978-1-5127-2636-7 (e)

Library of Congress Control Number: 2016900347

Print information available on the last page.

WestBow Press rev. date: 01/14/2016

Contents

Dedication

This book is dedicated to Patt, my life's partner for more than a half century.

We married when I was a young Marine just 20 years old.

I thought I knew God, but I had been deceived. I wrote the following on the flight to Japan where I would serve for more than a year. The poem will confirm that I didn't know the Father, or His Son.

When you begin reading the poem, imagine you are in a jet fighter plane revving up at the end of the runway preparing for take off. Imagine further that you are deluded in thinking you are in full control of your destiny.

Evanescent Bondage

Tally Ho you winged' beast!
I'll make you mine to say the least
as you respond beneath my hand
to chase my zeal across the land.

You'll take me up to skies unknown
where earthlings' seeds have not been sown
to make my home where jet streams tread
on the scimitar'd peak of the thunderhead.

And on my way to God's own lair
with pounding heart I'll speak this prayer:

"My Father God I come to Thee
to thank Thee for this endless sea
of cloud and wind where men weren't born.

But earthly bonds my mind has torn
that I might leave those worldly things
to seek Thy face on gifted wings.

Though thankful for this wing that lifts
I thank Thee more for perfect gifts...

for stemless cotton miles high
that paves my way across the sky...

for canyons lined with flawless white
and I, a man, to hold this sight!

Pray build me there a runway God
ten thousand long and not of sod,

then taxi me within Thy door
and chock me there forever more."

Through patience and devotion, Patt showed me that 'perfect gifts' were not beautiful clouds, but rather the Cross. She was both salt and light to me.

She was the epitome of the following.

"Wives...be submissive to your own husbands, that even if some do not obey the word, they, without a word, may be won by the conduct of their wives, when they observe your chaste conduct accompanied by fear. Do not let your adornment be merely outward...rather let it be the hidden person of the heart, with the incorruptible beauty of a gentle and quiet spirit..."
1 Peter 3:1-4 NKJV

Now 41 years past the time of my salvation, I still have an insatiable appetite to study and teach God's word.

After meeting Jesus my poems portrayed a different level of wisdom. The following summarizes the journey from my troubled teen years to the present.

When in the springtime of my life
no dream did I preclude.
I planned my seasons from my youth
in total solitude.

I had no knowledge of the One
who formed and fashioned me.
I lived my days for me alone
in vain hypocrisy.

For what the world could offer me
I traded for my soul
as wounds inflicted in my youth
began to take their toll.

But when my years were thirty-four
I heard my God proclaim,
"Before I made the universe
I called you by your name."

"I healed your wounds in former days
upon the rugged tree,
but you need reap what you had sown
before I set you free."

The summer solstice of my life
has given way to fall
as autumn beckons shorter days
per ancient protocol.

As falling leaves lay bare the trees
full knowledge will it bring
that what was once my fondest dream
had been fulfilled in spring.

Thank you, Patt. Because of your endurance we'll be together forever. And by the way, isn't 'together' a beautiful word.

Now also when I am old and gray headed, Oh God,
Do not forsake me, until I declare Your strength
To this generation, Your power
To everyone who is to come.
~~Proverbs~~ 71:18 NKJV
PSALMS

Chapter 1

Precursors to Adam

The odyssey of God's chosen becomes even more meaningful and interesting when one examines events that happened before Adam and the Garden of Eden. Borrowing a definition from Webster, the word 'precursor' as used in the title means 'someone or something that precedes and indicates the approach of something more.'

The first three words in the book of Genesis are 'In the beginning' and the Hebrew base for 'beginning' also means 'first.' Therefore, those initial three words confirm there were events or happenings that preceded the events recorded beginning with Genesis 1:2.

There are other phrases in the Bible that confirm the existence of and the working of the mind of God prior to man's physical creation. For example the phrases 'before time began' and 'from the foundation of the world' are also found in the Bible.

The first three words in the New Testament are exactly the same as the first three words in the Old Testament, i.e. 'In the beginning.' The Greek base for beginning also means 'first' and 'before anything.'

"In the beginning was the Word, and the Word was with God, and the Word was God. He was in the beginning with God." John 1:1 NIV

This verse clearly ascribes deity to Jesus.

The Greek base for 'Word' means the eternal expression of the divine intelligence and the disclosure of the divine essence.

The Pharisees would not accept Jesus' claim to deity. They boasted of their status and security by claiming they were direct descendants of Abraham.

"'I tell you the truth,' Jesus answered, 'before Abraham was born, I am!'" John 8:58 NIV

The term 'I am' means 'I have always been.'

The redemptive plan for man, particularly for gentiles via the church through the God/man Jesus, was not fully revealed until the New Testament. The Apostle Paul taught that such a plan had been devised 'in the beginning' or 'since the world began.'

"Now to Him who is able to establish you according to my gospel and the preaching of Jesus Christ, according to the revelation of the mystery kept secret since the world began, but now made manifest..." Romans 16:25-26a NKJV

The Greek base for 'world began' in the present context is *chronois aioniois* which means 'before time began.'

The very next chapter in the Bible reveals that the wisdom of God was/is embodied in Christ.

"...but we preach Christ crucified: a stumbling block to Jews and foolishness to Gentiles, but to those whom God has called, both Jews and Greeks, Christ the power of God and the wisdom of God." 1 Corinthians 1:23-24 NIV

The Greek for wisdom in this verse means divine wisdom, infinite skill, insight, and purity.

The Bible also reveals that wisdom was with God, 'in the beginning,' or before He prepared the earth to sustain Adam and all mankind.

Solomon declared that wisdom's greatest delight was to be with God's highest creation, i.e. those created in God's own image.

"I was there when he set the heavens in place...when He marked out the foundations of the earth. Then I was the craftsman at his side. I was filled with delight day after day...rejoicing in his whole world and delighting in mankind." Proverbs 8:27a, 29b-31 NIV

One cannot grasp the love that God has for His Son and for those whom He would create in His own image.

There are other great Biblical truths that tell of God's detailed preparation and plan for those whom He was about to create and place on the earth.

God's plan for man began long before the dimension of time and the Garden of Eden and will last long after, when time will be needed no more.

Angels in the order of creation

The Bible reveals that Jesus and wisdom were present in the beginning. The Bible further reveals that angels were created after the beginning but before Adam.

The Bible further reveals that angels were created not only to serve God but to minister to man who would subsequently be created in God's image. Angels would also execute judgment on the disobedient.

The greatest of the created angels was Lucifer, son of the morning.

"You were anointed as a guardian cherub, for so I ordained you...You were blameless in your ways from the day you were created till wickedness was found in you." Ezekiel 28:14-15 NIV

The wickedness found in Lucifer was pride and subsequent rebellion against his Creator.

"You said in your heart, 'I will ascend to heaven; I will raise my throne above the stars of God...I will make myself like the Most High.' But you are brought down to the grave, to the depths of the pit." Isaiah 14:13-15 NIV

The Bible describes the other angels that were created before man as 'morning stars' and 'sons of God.'

Recall when God interrogated Job:

"Where were you when I laid the earth's foundation? ...while the morning stars sang together, and all the angels (sons of God) shouted for joy?" Job 38:4, 7 NIV

The Bible indicates that many other angels followed Lucifer in his rebellion. In fact the Bible states that when Lucifer lost his place of authority in heaven he drew a third of the angels with him.

"And the angels who did not keep their positions of authority but abandoned their own home – these he has kept in darkness, bound with everlasting chains for judgment on the great Day." Jude 6 NIV

The Apostle Peter recorded the same truth, as he was describing future judgment.

"For if God did not spare angels when they sinned, but sent them to hell, putting them into gloomy dungeons to be held for judgment..." 2 Peter 2:4 NIV

The Greek for 'hell' in this verse is *tartaroo* and is the place where fallen angels or demons are confined. It is synonymous with the bottomless pit or the abyss.

A sober truth is that fallen angels are condemned forever, i.e. there is no provision for redemption for them. The lake of fire was created specifically for fallen angels and their leader.

When Jesus returns to earth after the tribulation and judges the nations, the redeemed will "…inherit the kingdom prepared for you from the foundation of the world…" but the unredeemed will be reserved for eternal condemnation designed for Satan and his followers.

"...Depart from me, you who are cursed, into the eternal fire prepared for the devil and his angels." Matthew 25:41 NIV

While Satan lost his position in heaven, he has been given the title and position of prince of this world. He still has access to the throne, however, to accuse redeemed man. But even that access will be lost resulting from the war with Michael and his angels.

"The great dragon was hurled down – that ancient serpent called the devil, or Satan, who leads the whole world astray. He was hurled to the earth, and his angels with him." Revelation 12:9 NIV

The spirits of the angels who followed Satan are demons. Many demons are chained in the abyss while many others are allowed to roam on the earth serving their leader until their final judgment.

"The sixth angel poured out his bowl on the great river Euphrates...Then I saw three evil spirits that looked like frogs; they came out of the mouth of the dragon...They are spirits of demons..." Revelation 16:12-14a NIV

During the time prior to their judgment, demons are subject not only to Christ but to powerful good angels, such as the sixth angel described in the above passage.

Therefore, the powerful but fallen angel Lucifer was created before God prepared the earth for Adam and his descendants. All other angels were also created before Genesis 1:2.

Angels were created both to minister to and chastise man, who would later be created in the very image of God.

Angels are very powerful beings but are lower than redeemed man.

"Do you not know that the saints will judge the world? ...Do you not know that we will judge angels?" 1 Corinthians 6:2-3 NIV

It is very interesting to learn how much God did in preparation for man.

God's eternal, immutable plan for His chosen

God's purpose for man was determined long before earth was prepared to sustain him. And while the plan was initially mentioned in the early chapters of Genesis, many details were shrouded in mystery until the earthly arrival of Jesus.

"All these things Jesus spoke to the multitude in parables... saying: 'I will open My mouth in parables, I will utter things kept secret from the foundation of the world.'" Matthew 13:34-35 NKJV

Parallel phrases for 'the foundation of the world' include 'the beginning of the creation,' or 'absolute beginning.' That confirms the truth that God's plan for man was devised long before God created him from dust.

Several times the Apostle Paul spoke of the mystery kept through many generations and reserved for God's chosen. The mystery would not be revealed to those of the world but rather for the glory of God's elect.

"We do, however, speak a message of wisdom among the mature, but not the wisdom of this age or of the rulers of this age, who are coming to nothing. No, we speak of God's secret wisdom, a wisdom that has been hidden and that God destined for our glory before time began. None of the rulers of this age understood it..." 1 Corinthians 2:6-8a NIV

The mystery revealed to the church was the gift of redemption made possible by the vicarious sacrifice of Christ.

"Therefore do not be ashamed of the testimony of our Lord...who has saved us...not according to our works, but according to His own purpose and grace which was given to us in Christ Jesus before time began, but has now been revealed..." 2 Timothy 1:8-10a NKJV

Paul also used the phrase 'before time began' when writing to Titus, confirming that God promised eternal life to His elect before the beginning of time.

"Paul, a bondservant of God and an apostle of Jesus Christ, according to the faith of God's elect and the acknowledgment of the truth which accords with godliness, in hope of eternal life which God, who cannot lie, promised before time began, but has in due time manifested His word..." Titus 1:1-3 NKJV

And to the church at Colosse he wrote:

"...the mystery that has been kept hidden for ages and generations, but is now disclosed to the saints." Colossians 1:26 NIV

And in Paul's letter to the church at Ephesus he expounded on the origin of God's plan and its contents.

"...this grace was given me...to make plain to everyone the administration of this mystery, which for ages past was kept hidden in God...His intent was that now, through the church, the manifold wisdom of God should be made known to the rulers and authorities...according to his eternal purpose which he accomplished in Christ Jesus our Lord." Ephesians 3:8-11 NIV

The term 'eternal' means 'without beginning or end.'

The Prophet Isaiah had previously revealed much about the eternal aspect of God.

"Who has done this and carried it through, calling forth the generations from the beginning? I, the Lord – with the first of them and with the last – I am he." Isaiah 41:4 NIV

The Hebrew for 'first' encompasses two aspects, i.e. beginning as related to time, and preeminence. The term 'last' means the One to bring the termination of the age.

"...I am God, and there is no other...I make known the end from the beginning, from ancient times, what is still to come. I say: 'My purpose will stand, and I will do all that I please.'" Isaiah 46:9-10 NIV

"Yes, and from ancient days I am he." Isaiah 43:13a NIV

The Psalmist also spoke of the eternal attribute of God.

"Before the mountains were born or you brought forth the earth and the world, from everlasting to everlasting you are God." Psalm 90:2 NIV

Therefore, there was much activity before the earth was prepared for man, and there will be much more activity after the end of this age.

And since Jesus is deity, He is likewise the 'first and the last.'

"I am the Alpha and the Omega, the First and the Last, the Beginning and the End." Revelation 22:13 NIV

In both Hebrew and Greek 'end' and 'last' can be used interchangeably.

Thus, God's plan for His elect was devised before time began and will never end. His plan was not made known to the Prophets; rather His plan was a mystery until revealed with the arrival of Christ and the establishment of the 'church.'

The fulfillment of God's plan for man is still in its early stages.

God's chosen and His registry

It has been determined that God's plan for His chosen was devised before the foundation of the world, or long before He breathed life into Adam. In fact those creation activities beginning with Genesis 1:2 were the beginning of the implementation of His eternal plan for man.

Many shun the concept of predestination. They feel that everyone has complete freedom to choose their future. Both positions are true, i.e. predestination and free choice are entirely compatible.

The Bible reveals that not only was God's plan for man devised from the foundation of the world, so were the participants of His plan.

"Praise be to the God and Father of our Lord Jesus Christ, who has blessed us in the heavenly realms with every spiritual blessing in Christ. For he chose us in him before the creation of the world..." Ephesians 1:3-4a NIV

Following are more details about the plan itself.

"...to be holy and blameless in his sight. In love he predestined us to be adopted as his sons through Jesus Christ, in accordance with his pleasure and will..." Ephesians 1:4b-5 NIV

God's plan for His chosen was to adopt them as sons by the sacrifice of His own son, and the reason was solely because He desired to do so.

Paul goes on to confirm God's purpose for His elect.

"In him we were also chosen, having been predestined according to the plan of him who works out everything

in conformity with the purpose of his will..." Ephesians 1:11 NIV

The Greek base for 'predestine' is to determine or decree beforehand. Then when writing to the Christians in Rome, Paul tells of both the eternal plan as well as the eternal participants.

"For those God foreknew he also predestined to be conformed to the likeness of his Son...and those he predestined, he also called; those he called, he also justified; those he justified, he also glorified." Romans 8:29-30 NIV

Note again the past tense of the verbs foreknew, predestined, justified, and glorified. According to God's master plan, God's chosen are between justified and glorified; and since 'glorified' is in the past tense, there is no way to prevent that event from becoming reality.

God's overall purpose is for His chosen ones to be conformed to the image of His Son.

The term 'foreknew' in the above context means 'foreordained.' In other words it defines those events that God deliberately ordained in eternity past for His purpose which will last through eternity future.

In eternity past prior to the creation activities beginning in Genesis 1:2, God recorded the names of His chosen in a registry.

The registry of God's chosen participants is called the Book of Life.

The Bible states specifically that the Book of Life was prepared before time began.

When the anti-Christ makes his appearance during the tribulation period, great power will be given to him to perform God's will. All people from all nations whose names were not recorded in the Book of Life will bow down and worship him.

"All inhabitants of the earth will worship the beast – all whose names have not been written in the book of life belonging to the Lamb that was slain from the creation of the world." Revelation 13:8 NIV

This powerful verse confirms that not only was the Book of Life filled at the foundation of the world, but the slaying of the Lamb of God was also foreordained from the foundation of the world.

The reality is, however, that not everyone is named in the Book of Life. Recall Jesus' teaching, relative to the saved.

"...For wide is the gate and broad is the road that leads to destruction...But small is the gate and narrow the road that leads to life, and only a few find it." Matthew 7:13-14 NIV

Those whose names are not in the Book will stand before God at the great white throne.

"And I saw the dead, small and great, standing before the throne, and books were opened...The dead were judged according to what they had done as recorded in the books." Revelation 20:12 NIV

Those not recorded in the Book of Life had rejected God's remedy for sin. That remedy was the vicarious death of Jesus.

"Another book was opened, which is the book of life...If anyone's name was not found written in the book of life, he was thrown into the lake of fire." Revelation 20:12, 15 NIV

Such was/is God's plan for His chosen.

Chapter 2

God's Eternal Plan takes Shape

The very first verse in the Bible states the earth was created in the beginning. The second verse states:

"Now the earth was formless and empty, darkness was over the surface of the deep..." Genesis 1:2a NIV

The Hebrew word for 'darkness' as used in the present context is *choshekh* which means 'figuratively blindness' or 'to be obscure.' For example:

"In that day...the eyes of the blind shall see out of obscurity and out of darkness." Isaiah 29:18 NKJV

In God's perfect ageless plan, for those whom He was soon to create in His own image, He was preparing to implement that matchless plan.

"...and the Spirit of God was hovering over the waters." Genesis 1:2b NIV

The Hebrew for 'Spirit' is wind and the same Hebrew word is used in the following:

"...and he sent a wind over the earth..." Genesis 8:1b NIV

And so it was, God visited the desolate earth.

"And God said, 'Let there be light,' and there was light." Genesis 1:3 NIV

The term 'light' in the present context is from the Hebrew *or* meaning 'illumination' or 'enlightenment.' Light is also associated with life, wisdom, and justice. The Hebrew meaning of light in the present context also represents God's glory.

If the preparation of the earth for man began with God providing light, why then, were the solar and lunar systems required?

"And God said, 'Let there be lights in the expanse of the sky to separate the day from the night, and let them serve as signs to mark seasons and days and years...to give light on the earth.'" Genesis 1:14-15 NIV

The Hebrew base for 'light' in the above verse is *maor* meaning a luminous body or a lamp.

One's first thought when noting the word 'seasons' in the above might be the four seasons experienced by the earth being tilted on its axis 23.5 degrees as it makes its annual journey around the sun.

However, a more specific meaning is revealed from the Hebrew *moedh* which means 'festive gathering, appointment, or signal.' It was to signal the timing of the subsequent Jewish feast days which would be revealed in due time.

The Hebrew for 'days' in Genesis 1:14 means 'time,' either between two points on the linear time span or a specific point of time on that span. The Hebrew word for 'year(s)' means a 'revolution of time,' or 'to return,' and/or 'repeat.' Such describes the earth's annual journey around the sun which defines a year.

The concept of time would be necessary to appreciate the grandeur of God's word as He lays out history in advance and ascribes specific measures of time to future events.

After God prepared the earth to sustain life, i.e. land, sea, and sky, He created Adam.

"Then God said, 'Let us make man in our image... let them rule over the fish of the sea and the birds of the air, over the livestock, over all the earth,' ...So God created man in his own image...male and female he created them. God blessed them and said to them, 'Be fruitful and increase in number; fill the earth and subdue it.'" Genesis 1:26-28a NIV

After God created man and every provision to sustain him, He was very satisfied and approved of all He had done.

"God saw all that he had made, and it was very good." Genesis 1:31a NIV

The Hebrew for 'very' means 'exceedingly.'

Man created in the image of God is the highest of God's creations. God's plan for man, which He devised countless years before He brought it into being, had now begun.

The subsequent journey would be endless and the result will be as originally intended, i.e. to fulfill God's purpose. The journey will prove man's ineptness without his Creator and simultaneously reveal God's holiness, righteousness, justice, longsuffering, and love.

It will take millennia for man to come to the realization that he can't do it on his own, if in fact he ever realizes it. Those that accept man's impotence and those that don't, define the two categories of all mankind.

How long will the earth last?

According to Genesis 1:1, the earth was created in the ageless past. The earth was subsequently made fit to sustain man and life as we know it beginning in Genesis 1:2. Many wonder how long the earth will last. According to President Obama, if America doesn't decrease her carbon footprint in this generation, the earth is doomed.

First, let's confirm the purpose of the earth.

"The heaven, even the heavens, are the LORD's; but the earth He has given to the children of men." Psalm 115:16 NKJV

The term 'children' above is the same Hebrew word used for 'sons' in the following referring to the object of wisdom's delight.

"...rejoicing in His inhabited world, and my delight was with the sons of men." Proverbs 8:31 NKJV

Sons (children) of men differentiate mankind from angels which are referred to as 'sons of God.'

Several times Psalmists confirmed the relationship of man to the earth.

"Who is the man that fears the LORD? ...his descendants shall inherit the earth." Psalm 25:12-13 NKJV

"...but those who wait on the LORD, they shall inherit the earth...the meek shall inherit the earth." Psalm 37:9, 11 NKJV

The Hebrew for 'inherit' means 'to take possession, occupy, or to be an heir.' The Hebrew for 'meek' means 'gentle, humble, and lowly.'

And in the New Testament Jesus, once again, confirmed Old Testament truths in His opening statements on His famous Sermon on the Mount.

"Blessed are the meek, for they shall inherit the earth." Matthew 5:5 NIV

It has been established that man will never cease to be, but how about planet earth?

"Forever, O LORD, Your word is settled in heaven... You established the earth, and it abides." Psalm 119:89-90 NKJV

The word 'abides' means 'stand' or 'remain.'

Perhaps the wisest man in the world said it best:

"Generations come and generations go, but the earth remains forever." Ecclesiastes 1:4 NIV

Therefore, both mankind and the earth will forever remain. However, both will undergo drastic renewal.

All mankind will be changed at their respective resurrections and the earth will undergo tremendous changes when it is renewed.

Isaiah referred to the changes to the earth as the 'new earth.'

"Behold, I will create new heavens and a new earth. The former things will not be remembered, nor will they come to mind." Isaiah 65:17 NIV

"As the new heavens and the new earth that I make will endure before me..." Isaiah 66:22 NIV

Once again these profound Scripture passages are confirmed in the New Testament; this time taught by Peter.

"But in keeping with his promises we are looking forward to a new heaven and a new earth, the home of righteousness." 2 Peter 3:13 NIV

The Greek meaning of the word 'new' means 'new in quality' or basically, 'renewal of the same physical object.'

The Apostle John was also given a vision of the future of the earth.

"Then I saw a new heaven and a new earth, for the first heaven and the first earth had passed away..." Revelation 21:1 NIV

Recall the two concepts of 'light' found in the first chapter of Genesis. Light as referenced in Genesis 1:3 meant 'enlightenment.' The light provided by the sun in Genesis 1:14 referred to a luminous body or lamp.

The same two sources of light are referenced in the final chapter of the Bible.

"There will be no more night. They will not need the light of a lamp or the light of the sun, for the Lord God will give them light. And they will reign forever and ever."
Revelation 22:5 NIV

Therefore, mankind, the earth, and light shall never cease to be.

While speaking at the European Space Agency recently renowned astrophysicist Stephen Hawking offered his take on the subject.

"Our planet is an old world, threatened with an ever-expanding population and finite resources. We must anticipate these threats and have a plan B. If our species is to survive the next hundred years, let alone a thousand, it is imperative we voyage out into the blackness of space to colonize new worlds across the cosmos."

The two opposing views of the future are quite different.

Everyone has the freedom to choose their own perspective.

From plan to substance

God's ageless plan for the earth and its future overseer takes on physical form. It began with light which revealed the very presence of the Creator. Next, God spoke three layers into existence, i.e. the waters in the atmosphere, the waters covering the earth, and the layer in between. Then

He caused dry land to appear in the midst of the waters which defined the continents and the water separating them He called 'seas.'

On the dry land He caused foliage to appear which would yield fruit to sustain the life which He was about to create.

Then God created the solar and lunar systems, which would provide a means for future man to measure time and thereby understand history, which God was about to write before it actually unfolded.

Next God created life to fill the seas, the land, and the layer above the earth's surface for the birds.

And then the capstone of God's creation: God created man in His own image, as previously stated, to have dominion over all other life on the earth.

The second chapter of Genesis begins by stating that God's creative work for earth and man was completed.

"Thus the heavens and the earth were completed in all their vast array. By the seventh day God had finished the work he had been doing; so on the seventh day he rested from all his work." Genesis 2:1-2 NIV

There were seven 'days' in God's week to prepare the earth and its inhabitants to fulfill God's purpose for them.

It will be seen that God will use the number seven and its multiples to explain the mysteries of pre-written history.

It should also be noted that every living animal, bird, or fish was created and would multiply after 'its own kind.' That Biblical truth would seem to dispel the confidence in the school of thought commonly termed 'evolution.'

Up to that point in history, rain had not yet been provided; rather 'a mist went up from the earth and watered the whole face of the ground.' Also 'there was no man to till the ground.'

God had chosen a particular place on the earth where He would place His ultimate creation.

"The LORD God planted a garden eastward in Eden... and out of the ground the LORD God made every tree grow that is pleasant to the sight and good for food. The tree of life was also in the midst of the garden, and the tree of the knowledge of good and evil." Genesis 2:8-9 NKJV

God provided flowing rivers to water the garden which contained the tree of life. The location of the Garden would subsequently be called Babylon in the land of Shinar. The location is presently called Iraq.

There were four rivers that provided water for the Garden, two of which were the Tigris and Euphrates.

The next step in the sequence was to place His highest creation in the midst of the garden to 'tend and keep' it. In other words man would be given the responsibility to assist in the earth's productivity, to fulfill the purpose which God had determined before time began.

Man's journey would soon begin with a simple, single instruction to test his obedience.

Introducing God's steward for the earth

We've seen that man was created in God's image to have dominion over the earth and all other life on the earth. What makes man unique with respect to other living creatures?

"The Lord God formed the man from the dust of the ground and breathed into his nostrils the breath of life, and the man became a living being." Genesis 2:7 NIV

There are three terms used relative to Adam's origin. It was stated previously that Adam was created in the image of God. 'Created' means 'to be brought into existence from nothing,' i.e. to be initiated which can only be done by an act of God. 'Made' means 'to construct, build, fulfill for a purpose' while 'formed' similarly means 'to fashion for a predestined purpose.'

Recall that God looked on His work on earth after He created Adam and described it as 'very good.' 'Very' does mean 'exceedingly' as previously stated, but other synonyms include 'utterly and wholly.' The term 'good' means 'excellent, fruitful, and righteous.'

Jesus expounded on the term 'good' in His teachings while addressing the rich young ruler.

"'*Why do you call me good?' Jesus Answered. 'No one is good – except God alone.'*" Luke 18:19 NIV

Therefore, Adam was created, made, and formed with Godlike attributes. (IMAGE)

In Genesis 2:7 above it states that God formed man… and breathed into his nostrils the breath of life so that Adam became a living being.

The Hebrew for 'breath' means the 'Spirit of God' including wisdom and divine inspiration. 'Life' in the phrase 'breath of life' means 'to live forever' and 'fresh running water.' In the KJV the term 'soul' is used instead of life with meanings including 'spirit and mind.' Death occurs when 'life' departs.

The term 'life' in the phrase 'tree of life' is from the same Hebrew base used in 'breath of life' in Genesis 2:7. In other words, the tree of life was meant to sustain Adam and his descendants with life as defined above forever.

Adam was endowed with more than the imagination could ever dream of.

In His infinite wisdom God observed in His timing that while Adam named and had dominion over all other living creatures, he had no mate comparable to himself. The terminology in the KJV is 'but for Adam there was not found a help meet for him.'

The word 'help' in the above means 'aid.'

The phrase 'meet for him' in the Hebrew means 'part opposite,' specifically a 'counterpart' or 'mate.'

Adam was provided a perfectly suited mate.

"So the LORD God caused the man to fall into a deep sleep; and while he was sleeping, he took one of the man's ribs and closed up the place with flesh. Then the LORD God made a woman from the rib..." Genesis 2:21-22 NIV

When God brought the woman to Adam, Adam said:

"This is now bone of my bones and flesh of my flesh..." Genesis 2:23 NIV

The woman, subsequently named Eve, was of the exact species of Adam. She was, however, the counterpart of Adam. A proper definition of counterpart is 'something that fits another perfectly; something that completes; one remarkably similar to another.' While Adam was a man Eve was a woman. Adam was a male and Eve was a female.

"For this reason a man will leave his father and mother and be united to his wife, and they will become one flesh." Genesis 2:24 NIV

That was/is God's plan for man to 'be fruitful and multiply; fill the earth, and subdue it...'

God's perfect plan and perfect relationship for Adam and Eve had begun. They were placed in perfect surroundings and in fact were in the very presence of God Himself. It couldn't have been any better.

The couple that had everything

Adam and Eve were created/made in the very image of God. They lived in a wonderful place in the very presence of God. They had been given stewardship over every living creature on land, air, and sea. They were created to live forever. They could want for nothing.

Inasmuch as God created/made them, He had complete authority over them to set any conditions He deemed necessary for their benefit and protection. And there was only one condition He set to measure their obedience.

"The LORD God took the man and put him in the Garden of Eden to work it and take care of it. And the LORD God commanded the man, 'You are free to eat from any tree in the garden; but you must not eat from the tree

of the knowledge of good and evil, for when you eat of it you will surely die.'" Genesis 2:15-17 NIV

The single condition was very basic and straightforward. They could partake of all trees in the garden including the tree of life, but not of the tree of the knowledge of good and evil. Not only was this a test of their obedience; there was no reason for them to know 'evil.'

The Hebrew for 'die' in the present context means physical death. Synonyms include 'kill' and 'slay.' Physical death was a major consequence of the curse directed towards Adam, i.e. *"and to dust you shall return."* The writer of Hebrews confirmed such death, *"And it is appointed for men to die once..."*

Now Satan was well aware of God's requirement on Adam and Eve. He had just one opportunity to disrupt the perfect plan and he took full advantage of that opportunity.

"Now the serpent was more cunning than any beast of the field, which the LORD God had made. And he said to the woman, 'Has God indeed said,' "You shall not eat of every tree of the garden?"'" Genesis 3:1 NKJV

The term 'serpent' does indeed mean 'snake;' however, the serpent appeared as one to shed light on God's command. Eve didn't recognize the serpent for who he really was.

Recall the instruction not to partake of the tree of the knowledge of good and evil was originally given to Adam.

Adam in turn had relayed the command to Eve. The serpent approached Eve, who as Adam's counterpart was more susceptible to being deceived.

The Hebrew for 'cunning' means 'subtle, sly, and/or crafty.' The serpent's subtlety exceeded that of any other of God's created beasts on the earth.

Eve responded to the serpent's question.

"The woman said to the serpent, 'We may eat fruit from the trees in the garden, but God did say, You must not eat fruit from the tree that is in the middle of the garden, and you must not touch it, or you will die.'" Genesis 3:2-3 NIV

The serpent responded with 'logic,' saying there was no reason for God to place any restrictions on their freedom in the garden. The serpent convinced Eve that she would actually benefit from eating the fruit.

And so it was.

"When the woman saw that the fruit of the tree was good for food and pleasing to the eye, and also desirable for gaining wisdom, she took some and ate it. She also gave some to her husband, who was with her, and he ate it." Genesis 3:6 NIV

Eve saw only the perceived benefits of eating the forbidden fruit. A key term in the above passage is 'desirable.' It is the Hebrew *chamadh* which is translated 'covet.' It means 'to long for.' It represents an inordinate, ungoverned, selfish desire. The same Hebrew word is the basis of the 10th Commandment, i.e. 'You shall not covet…'

One of the results of their disobedience was recognition of their sinful state. They attempted to cover their nakedness by clothing themselves with fig leaves.

Because of God's holiness all disobedience must be dealt with. When He confronted Adam, Adam pointed to Eve. Eve in turn blamed her disobedience on the serpent.

"The woman said, 'The serpent deceived me, and I ate.'" Genesis 3:13b NIV

The consequences would be devastating.

One sin changed the world

The consequence of the single sin of disobedience did, in fact, change the world. While Eve was deceived into the sin, Adam consciously ate of the fruit which God had instructed him not to eat thereof.

When confronted with the sin of disobedience Eve offered the defense that the serpent had deceived her. The original KJV uses the term 'beguiled.' In both cases the meaning is 'to be led astray, deluded, and/or seduced.' When the results are expressed as a noun, synonyms include a lie or sham resulting in perjury.

Paul in the New Testament revealed that the serpent's methods of deceit in Genesis are alive and active in the present age. He reminded the church at Corinth of false apostles.

"For such men are false apostles, deceitful workmen, masquerading as apostles of Christ. And no wonder, for Satan himself masquerades as an angel of light (enlightenment)." 2 Corinthians 11:13-14 NIV

The initial sin of disobedience in the garden was/is the cause of the curse that pervades the present age. The curse was to affect the serpent, the woman, the man, and in effect the entire earth.

The serpent was cursed above all other beasts of the field. He would henceforth crawl on his belly in the dust.

The most significant part of the curse, however, affected the one who presented himself to Eve as an angel of light, i.e. Satan himself. Recall his description in the final book of the Bible:

"– that ancient serpent called the devil, or Satan, who leads the whole world astray..." Revelation 12:9 NIV

The curse given to the devil introduced the response of the Creator to the devil's actions.

"And I (God) will put enmity between you and the woman, and between your seed and her Seed; He shall

bruise your head, and you shall bruise His heel." Genesis 3:15 NKJV

Notice the absolute sovereignty of God as He proclaims: 'I will.'

The Hebrew term for bruise means 'overwhelm, crush, or break.' 'Head' means 'foremost, supreme, or highest,' while 'heel' means basically a 'protuberant' or nonessential part.

In other words, the Seed of the woman would one day in God's precise timing totally destroy the enemy, the very one who deceived her. Her very offspring, i.e. in the form of flesh and blood would destroy the most powerful enemy of God and man.

The curse directed to the woman included pain in childbearing and conflict with her mate. While she was originally made to be a partner to Adam, she would now be required to be submissive to his headship. This newly defined role would cause tension between husband and wife, as she would lose her heretofore independence.

The curse directed to Adam included toil and effort in all his endeavors, as well as death, both physical and spiritual.

"For since death came through a man, the resurrection of the dead comes also through a man. For as in Adam all

die, so in Christ all will be made alive..." 1 Corinthians 15:21-22 NIV

The term 'die' in the above is from the Greek *apollumi* meaning 'eternal death.' And Christ is the Seed of the woman first mentioned in Genesis 3:15.

And so it was Adam and Eve were expelled from the Garden of Eden. They lost access to the tree of life, which had been given to provide life to mankind forever. Death resulting from sin, however, was not to be the final destiny of God's chosen.

It must be noted that God provided more suitable clothing for Adam and Eve as they were expelled from the garden.

"The LORD God made garments of skin for Adam and his wife and clothed them." Genesis 3:21 NIV

Once again, the absolute sovereignty of God is revealed. 'He made' and 'He clothed' them.

The fact that He clothed them introduced the doctrine of the 'Righteousness Garment' which would be revealed at a later time.

And most significantly, the fact that God clothed them with the skins of animals before expelling them from the garden signifies that innocent blood was shed to cover the sin of Adam and Eve.

God's immutable plan of redemption had begun!

The enmity begins

Recall the proclamation against Satan after he deceived Eve in the garden.

"And I will put enmity between you and the woman, and between your seed and her Seed..." Genesis 3:15 NKJV

Firstly it is noted that God said, "I will put..." In other words the enmity between Satan and the woman, and his descendants and her Seed, would be initiated by God to execute his plan devised from the foundation of the world. Synonyms for 'enmity' include 'hostility, adversarial, hatred,' i.e. 'to be foes.'

After Adam and Eve were expelled from the garden clothed in animal skins, they had two sons.

"Adam lay with his wife Eve, and she became pregnant and gave birth to Cain. She said, 'With the help of the LORD I have brought forth a man.' Later she gave birth to his brother Abel. Now Abel kept flocks, and Cain worked the soil." Genesis 4:1-2 NIV

The two sons were very different. Abel was obedient while Cain was independently headstrong. Both knew God's desire for animal sacrifices; however, Cain chose to offer what he thought would be more fitting.

"And in the process of time it came to pass that Cain brought an offering of the fruit of the ground to the LORD.

Abel also brought of the firstborn of his flock and of their fat. And the LORD respected Abel and his offering but He did not respect Cain and his offering. And Cain was very angry..." Genesis 4:3-5 NKJV

The term 'respect' in the above means to 'inspect, consider,' and then have compassion on. In other words God was well pleased with Abel's offering of a sacrificial animal, but was not pleased with Cain's idea of an acceptable offering. As a result Cain was very angry. In Hebrew 'angry' or 'wroth' meant 'to be incensed or indignant.'

God asked Cain why he was angry. He told Cain that if he had obeyed instructions, all would have been well. He went on to say that sin desired to pounce on him but a blood sacrifice would protect and atone for, or expiate his sins.

"If you do what is right, will you not be accepted? But if you do not do what is right, sin is crouching at your door; it desires to have you, but you must master it." Genesis 4:7 NIV

The 'door' in the above means 'entrance or opening.' It also means to 'remove one's protection.'

It might have been expected that Cain would have listened and heeded God's instructions; however, such was not the case. Cain in his jealousy took revenge on his brother.

"...And while they were in the field, Cain attacked his brother Abel and killed him." Genesis 4:8b NIV

Cain was then cursed to be a vagabond and fugitive on the earth. 'Vagabond' and/or 'fugitive' are synonyms meaning 'to be a wanderer' or 'to flee.' He recognized that this curse was a punishment for his sin. The Hebrew for 'punishment' means 'the results of a depraved action, or perverseness.'

It is extremely important to note that Cain left God's presence and wandered to the east.

"So Cain went out from the LORD's presence and lived in the land of Nod, east of Eden." Genesis 4:16 NIV

'Nod' means 'exile' or 'vagrancy.' Much more will be said about the 'east' later.

The two first sons of Adam and Eve represent the enmity between Satan and the woman, and his seed and her seed. Cain is associated with evil while Abel is considered righteous.

"This is how we know who the children of God are and who the children of the devil are: Anyone who does not do what is right is not a child of God; nor is anyone who does not love his brother...We should love one another. Do not be like Cain, who belonged to the evil one and murdered his brother. And why did he murder him? Because his own actions were evil and his brother's were righteous." 1 John 3:10-12 NIV

The murder of righteous Abel by the seed of the 'evil one' was Satan's first attempt to destroy the lineage of the Seed of the woman.

The righteous son was killed leaving the son of the devil. The battle of good vs. evil had just begun.

Sons of the East

Cain, the firstborn of Adam and Eve, was in fact described later by John as 'of the wicked one.' Cain did not honor God's instructions relative to his offering; was angry because God confronted him on his actions; killed his brother Abel in jealousy, and subsequently became a vagabond and fugitive. Cain 'went out from the presence of the LORD and dwelt in the land...east of Eden.'

The term 'east' when used in the Old Testament typically means that land from Palestine to the Euphrates River. The specific context, however, may include Mesopotamia and Babylon, i.e. present day Iraq. Joshua also referred to the land on the other side of the 'river' meaning that land east of the Euphrates River. That definition could include present day Iran, Afghanistan, and Pakistan.

Several millennia after the time of Cain, Abraham was called by God to leave the land of the east and travel to a new land that God would reveal to him. That new land includes present day Israel.

Recall Abraham's first two sons: the son of promise, named Isaac; and the son of the flesh, named Ishmael. Ishmael and his mother subsequently departed from

Abraham and settled in Arabia, where he was the father of twelve tribes.

Abraham had other sons by his subsequent wife Keturah and concubines.

"Abraham left everything he owned to Isaac. But while he was still living, he gave gifts to the sons of his concubines and sent them away from his son Isaac to the land (country) of the east." Genesis 25:5-6 NIV

God used the 'sons of the east' to chastise Israel when needed.

"Then the children of Israel did evil in the sight of the LORD. So the LORD delivered them into the hand of Midian... and the hand of Midian prevailed against Israel... So it was, whenever Israel had sown, Midianites would come up; also Amalekites and the children of the East would come up against them." Judges 6:1, 3 NKJV

After the time of the Judges during the consolidated kingdom, Solomon was recognized by all to be the wisest man on earth.

"Solomon's wisdom was greater than the wisdom of all the men of the East..." 1 Kings 4:30 NIV

The Queen of Sheba, which is present day Yemen, openly declared Solomon's wisdom and made prophetic utterance.

"Praise be to the LORD your God, who has delighted in you and placed you on the throne of Israel. Because of the LORD's eternal love for Israel, he has made you king, to maintain justice and righteousness." 1 Kings 10:9 NIV

Her words were true when spoken, and will prove to be fulfilled in the future. In the present, however, it is difficult to imagine such a proclamation coming out of Yemen.

Progressing several hundred years after Solomon's reign, the prophet Isaiah confirmed the Queen's words.

The context of the following describes the return of the conquering Christ as He re-gathers the children of Israel and defeats their enemies.

"In that day the Root of Jesse will stand as a banner for the peoples; the nations will rally to him...He will raise a banner for the nations and gather the exiles of Israel; he will assemble the scattered people of Judah...together they will plunder the people of the east." Isaiah 11:10, 12, 14 NIV

And then approximately 700 years after that, the wise men from the East journeyed to Bethlehem to worship the new born King of Israel, i.e. the Root of Jesse. God had miraculously provided a star in the East for a sign of the arrival of Christ.

The Apostle John, in the final book in the Bible, provides the last prophecy regarding the sons of the East.

"The sixth angel poured out his bowl on the great river Euphrates, and its water was dried up to prepare the way for the kings from the East." Revelation 16:12 NIV

Therefore, the sons of the East are referenced throughout history: past, present, and future.

Chapter 3

God says "I Will…"

Even though man had unwittingly interfered with God's immutable plan, God charged on to fulfill it. Countless times in the Scriptures the words "I will" are spoken by God. Those two words indicate actions that God would take to accomplish His indescribable purpose and plan for His chosen.

The following includes just a small portion of the "I wills" included in the Bible; however, they represent several of the most significant proclamations that describe God's plan of redemption for man.

God reveals the struggle, the players, and the outcome

It begins with God revealing that the journey for man would include tremendous interference from the enemy. The battle between good and evil had begun. The winner; however, was announced at the very beginning.

"And I will put enmity between you and the woman, and between your seed and her Seed; He shall bruise your head, and you shall bruise His heel." Genesis 3:15 NKJV

This significant passage was referenced in chapter 2. In the present context the emphasis is on the phrase "I will." God would orchestrate the entire odyssey for man including the battle for his soul. The actions of the enemy would be totally within the limits granted by Almighty God.

The conflict was/is and will be very heavy for man, but the total journey is framed by the love that God has for His own.

A righteous man named Noah

After many generations of disobedience and the judgment of the flood, God said that such a judgment would never be repeated. Recall His words as He smelled the 'soothing aroma' of Noah's burnt offering.

"Then the LORD said in His heart, 'I will never again curse the ground for man's sake, although the imagination of man's heart is evil from his youth; nor will I again destroy every living thing as I have done.'" Genesis 8:21 NKJV

The "I wills" in this verse include that God would never again curse the ground and never again destroy every living thing, even though man's heart was evil by nature. This verse confirms God's steadfastness of purpose and His longsuffering towards those created in His own image.

As Genesis unfolded God revealed more details of how He would accomplish His purpose through a man named Noah and his three sons, i.e. Ham, Shem and Japeth.

Recall Ham's sin against his father and the subsequent curse directed towards his son Canaan.

"When Noah awoke from his wine and found out what his youngest son had done to him, he said, 'Cursed be Canaan! The lowest of slaves will he be to his brothers.' He also said, 'Blessed be the LORD, the God of Shem! May Canaan be the slave of Shem.'" Genesis 9:24-26 NIV

The Hebrew for 'Canaan' as used in the above has several interesting meanings including 'humiliated' and 'merchant,' i.e. 'to traffic.'

Enter Abram (Abraham)

God would call a man from the east named Abram, a descendant of Noah's son Shem. God told Abram to leave his native land where other gods were served and journey west to a new land that He would show him. This new land was Canaan, inhabited by the descendants of Ham, a son of Noah.

As God spoke to Abram, He, once again, spoke the words "I will" several times.

"I will make you a great nation; I will bless you and make your name great...I will bless those who bless you and I will curse him who curses you; and in you all the families of the earth shall be blessed." Genesis 12:2-3 NKJV

This passage introduces the concept of a nation. 'Nation' is the Hebrew *Goy* with synonyms including 'populace, people, or tribe.' The word 'family' in Hebrew is very closely related with the word 'nation.' A family is actually a subdivision of a nation.

Notice the "I wills." "I will make," "I will bless," "I will curse." God would implement His plan through Abram and his descendants and all mankind would experience either blessings or curses via Abram and his family. As of 2016 AD, nothing has changed.

Following the promise to Abram, another significant "I will" is revealed.

"Then the LORD appeared to Abram and said, 'To your descendants I will give this land.'" Genesis 12:7 NKJV

God said "I will give this land." The word 'land' also has several synonyms including country or nation. The above verse confirms the promise and inheritance of Abram's 'seed.' The Hebrew for 'descendant' is synonymous with 'seed.' The land that God would give to Abram and his descendants would reach to the River Euphrates.

Preparation before possession

Another significant "I will" is that God would judge those who would afflict His people. God told Abram in great detail what was planned for him.

"...Know for certain that your descendants will be strangers in a country not their own, and they will be enslaved and mistreated four hundred years. But I will punish the nation they serve as slaves, and afterward they will come out with great possessions." Genesis 15:13-14 NIV

God spoke to Abram with absolute certainty when Abram was 75 years old which was in approximately 2090 BC. It would be hundreds of years later, when Abram's grandson Jacob was an old man, that 71 of Abram's descendants would journey to Egypt to begin their foretold captivity. They would be redeemed four centuries later as a nation and begin their journey to the land promised them.

The "I will" is that God would judge Egypt for their treatment of Abram's family while in Egypt and during their Exodus from there.

Approximately 24 years later God appeared to Abram again with more details of his future.

"'I am God Almighty...I will confirm my covenant between me and you and will greatly increase your numbers.' Abram fell facedown, and God said to him, 'As

for me, this is my covenant with you: You will be the father of many nations. No longer will you be called Abram; your name will be Abraham, for I have made you a father of many nations. I will make you very fruitful; I will make nations of you, and kings will come from you. I will establish my covenant as an everlasting covenant between me and you and your descendants after you for the generations to come, to be your God and the God of your descendants after you. The whole land of Canaan, where you are now an alien, I will give as an everlasting possession to you and your descendants after you; and I will be their God.'" Genesis 17:1b-8 NIV

Significant "I wills" in this passage include "I will confirm my covenant between me and you," "I will greatly increase your numbers," "I will make you very fruitful," "I will make nations of you," and "I will be their (Abraham's descendants) God."

Other significant proactive phrases spoken by God include "I have made," and "I will give…"

Key confirmation points include that God's promises to Abraham and his descendants (seed) would be forever. Again God confirmed that man's future would be based on Abraham's past, i.e. his faith which was counted as righteousness. Man's only requirement would be obedience.

Abraham's two sons

Further in the same encounter God spoke of Abraham's wife's participation.

"And I will bless her and surely give you a son by her. I will bless her so that she will be the mother of nations; kings of peoples will come from her." Genesis 17:16 NIV

The words "I will bless her" are found twice in this verse. Of extreme significance is the promise that Abraham would father a son by her in her old age, i.e. 90 years old. Abraham had a difficult time with that promise and offered alternatives.

"Then God said... 'your wife Sarah will bear you a son, and you will call him Isaac. I will establish my covenant with him as an everlasting covenant for his descendants after him. And as for Ishmael, I have heard you: I will surely bless him; I will make him fruitful and will greatly increase his numbers. He will be the father of twelve rulers, and I will make him into a great nation. But my covenant I will establish with Isaac, whom Sarah will bear to you by this time next year.'" Genesis 17:19-21 NIV

Other significant instances of "I will" in the above include "I will establish My covenant with him (Isaac)," and to Ishmael, "I will make him fruitful..." and "I will make him into a great nation."

Ishmael was indeed blessed by God. He was the beginning of the Arab nations.

Again, everything is based on what God said He was going to do, i.e. "I will." Note also that God's covenant with Isaac would be everlasting while the promises to Ishmael were not.

It is also very significant that the promises made to Abraham were to pass on to Abraham's son Isaac, i.e. Abraham's seed through his wife Sarah. Isaac would be the son of promise, while Ishmael was the son born according to the flesh. That truth with its accompanying ramifications would be exemplified throughout the Scriptures.

Abraham is tested

Continuing on in Genesis, Abraham was told by God to offer his only son Isaac as a burnt offering. Abraham without question was prepared to do as God instructed, but when Isaac didn't see any animal for the offering he questioned his father. Abraham's response was profound and prophetic.

"God himself will provide the lamb for the burnt offering, my son." Genesis 22:8 NIV

Just as Abraham took the knife to slay his only son, the Angel of the LORD called out to him.

"...because you have done this and have not withheld your son, your only son, I will surely bless you and make your descendants as numerous as the stars in the sky and as the sand on the seashore...and through your offspring all nations on earth will be blessed, because you have obeyed me." Genesis 22:16-18 NIV

God considered that Abraham had but one son, i.e. the son of promise named Isaac.

The Angel of the LORD said, "I will surely bless you," and "I will make your descendants as numerous as the stars in the sky..." And the Angel reiterated that in Abraham's seed all the nations of the earth would be blessed because of his obedience.

God confirms His promise to Abraham's seed, i.e. Isaac and Jacob

Shortly thereafter the same promises were given directly to Isaac. The LORD said, "I will be with you," "I will perform the oath..." "I will make your descendants multiply..." and "I will give your descendants all these lands." At that time God told Isaac that in his seed all the nations of the earth would be blessed because his father Abraham had obeyed God.

And then God spoke directly to Isaac's son, i.e. Abraham's grandson, Jacob and confirmed His plan for Israel and all mankind.

"I am the LORD, the God of your father Abraham and the God of Isaac. I will give you and your descendants the land on which you are lying. Your descendants will be like the dust of the earth...All peoples on earth will be blessed through you and your offspring. I am with you and will watch over you wherever you go, and I will bring you back to this land. I will not leave you until I have done what I have promised you." Genesis 28:13-15 NIV

God made the same promises to Jacob, "I will give you…the land," "I am with you and will watch over you…," "I will bring you back…," and "I will not leave you…" And again through Jacob and his seed all the nations of the earth will be blessed.

God subsequently appeared to Jacob a second time and confirmed His promises. This time He changed Jacob's name.

"God said to him, 'Your name is Jacob, but you will no longer be called Jacob; your name will be Israel.' So he named him Israel." Genesis 35:10 NIV

Jacob's (Israel) servitude reaffirmed along with the promise of redemption

Near the end of the Book of Genesis as Jacob came to Beersheba on his journey to Egypt, God spoke with him once again.

"And God spoke to Israel in a vision at night and said, 'Jacob! Jacob!' 'Here I am,' he replied. 'I am God, the God of your father,' he said. 'Do not be afraid to go down to Egypt, for I will make you into a great nation there. I will go down to Egypt with you, and I will surely bring you back again.'" Genesis 46:2-4 NIV

God's promises of what He would do include "I will make you into a great nation," "I will go down to Egypt with you..." and "I will surely bring you back again..." Significant points include that God would make Israel a great nation while in Egypt and the surety of their deliverance from bondage'

The lineage of the 'Seed of the woman'

The book of Genesis is filled with proclamations made by God, detailing how He would fulfill His promise of redemption. One such significant statement was that the Redeemer would come through the lineage of Abraham, Isaac, Jacob, Judah...

Recall Jacob's words to his sons as he was nearing death in Egypt.

"Then Jacob called for his sons and said: 'Gather around so I can tell you what will happen to you in days to come (last days).'" Genesis 49:1 NIV

He then prophesied about each of his sons. Of particular interest were his prophetic words concerning Judah.

"The scepter will not depart from Judah, nor the ruler's staff from between his feet, until he comes to whom it belongs and the obedience of the nations is his...he will wash his garments in wine, his robes in the blood of grapes." Genesis 49:10-11 NIV

Jacob in the above passage foretold that Judah, and through his seed or offspring, would be the tribe to provide Israel's Redeemer/King and the day would come when Judah's Redeemer/King would destroy His enemies in bloody battle.

Genesis comes to an end with final words from Joseph, son of Jacob.

"I am...dying, but God will surely visit you, and bring you out of this land to the land of which He swore to Abraham, to Isaac, and to Jacob." Genesis 50:24 NKJV

The promise that God "will surely visit you," was given one last time and confirmed that Israel's redemption was a done deal.

After the fall in the Garden, God through many "I will" promises outlined His plan for redemption devised before the world ever was.

Key components of His plan of redemption included Abraham and his seed (descendants), the making of the nation named Israel, and the making of many other nations. These components will continue throughout history to facilitate God's redemptive plan which will continue into eternity.

Israel after redemption from Egypt

Four hundred and thirty years after Jacob's journey into Egypt, God spoke again using the words "I will," as 71 people had grown into a great nation.

"Therefore, say to the Israelites: 'I am the LORD, and I will bring you out from under the yoke of the Egyptians. I will free you from being slaves to them, and I will redeem you with an outstretched arm and with mighty acts of judgment. I will take you as my own people, and I will be your God. Then you will know that I am the LORD your God, who brought you out from under the yoke of the Egyptians. And I will bring you to the land I swore with uplifted hand to give to Abraham, to Isaac and to Jacob. I will give it to you as a possession. I am the LORD.'" Exodus 6:6-8 NIV

"I will bring you out...I will free you from being slaves, I will redeem you...I will take you as My own people...I will be your God...I will bring you to the land...I will give it to you as a possession..."

The enemy would labor to thwart God's plan of redemption by trying to prevent the Seed of the woman from being born. His plan was doomed from the beginning, and he would suffer humiliating and total defeat.

God's "I wills" would all become "I did."

What Gods says, that He will do

God has made tremendously profound proclamations of His intentions in implementing His plan of redemption for mankind.

Shortly before entering the land of Canaan, God spoke through a false prophet named Balaam.

"The LORD met with Balaam and put a message in his mouth... 'God is not a man, that he should lie, nor a son of man, that he should change his mind. Does he speak and then not act? Does he promise and not fulfill?'" Numbers 23:16, 19 NIV

The prophet Amos addressed the issue by stating that God issues warnings before He acts, so when He speaks, one had better prepare to take heed.

"Surely the Sovereign LORD does nothing without revealing his plan to his servants the prophets. The lion has roared – who will not fear? The Sovereign LORD has spoken – who can but prophesy?" Amos 3:7-8 NIV

Shortly thereafter, the prophet Isaiah confirmed the immutability of God's proclamations.

"'I am God, and there is none like me. I make known the end from the beginning, from ancient times, what is still to come.' I say: 'My purpose will stand, and I will do all that I please.'" Isaiah 46:9b-10 NIV

Not only does God declare the big picture in advance, He confirms that what He says He will do, He will do.

Isaiah then tells that God's word would accomplish the purpose for which it was spoken.

"...so is my word that goes out from my mouth: It will not return to me empty, but will accomplish what I desire and achieve the purpose for which I sent it." Isaiah 55:11 NIV

God speaks, and His words will be totally fulfilled. There are no idle words with God.

History has confirmed the truth that God's word, is and will be, totally fulfilled in His timing.

"So the LORD gave Israel all the land he had sworn to give their forefathers, and they took possession of it and settled there. The LORD gave them rest on every side, just as he had sworn to their forefathers. Not one of their enemies withstood them; the LORD handed all their enemies over to them. Not one of all the LORD's good promises to

the house of Israel failed; every one was fulfilled." Joshua 21:43-45 NIV

Advanced warnings

Joshua warns the Israelites that just as all the good things the LORD had promised came to pass, so will chastisement for disobedience.

"But just as every good promise of the LORD your God has come true, so the LORD will bring on you all the evil he has threatened, until he has destroyed you from this good land he has given you. If you violate the covenant of the LORD your God, which he commanded you...the LORD's anger will burn against you, and you will quickly perish from the good land he has given you." Joshua 23:15-16 NIV

And lastly, it is impossible for God to lie. The New Testament confirms the writers of the Old Testament relative to the immutability of God's word.

"Because God wanted to make the unchanging nature of his purpose very clear to the heirs of what was promised, he confirmed it with an oath. God did this so that, by two unchangeable things in which it is impossible for God to lie..." Hebrews 6:17-18 NIV

Therefore, when the lion roars, all had better take heed and proceed accordingly with total confidence.

Recall Jesus' words to His followers just prior to His ascension.

"This is what I told you while I was still with you: Everything must be fulfilled that is written about me in the Law of Moses, the Prophets and the Psalms." Luke 24:44 NIV

Therefore, God's plan of redemption for His chosen as outlined in the Scriptures can be embraced with total confidence.

Chapter 4

Introduction to Redemption

The doctrine of redemption is the most significant doctrine in the Bible. Redemption defines the path back from east of Eden to the presence of God.

When Adam and Eve were expelled from Eden, they had been consigned to die because of disobedience to their Creator. They were denied access to the tree of life; i.e. they had lost their right to life. Their sin would affect all mankind proceeding from them. Their descendants would be born without the Spirit of God.

"For as in Adam all die..." 1 Corinthians 15:22a NIV

The Greek for 'die' in this verse meant that death would be a natural and expected occurrence for all of mankind.

In order for Adam and Eve and their offspring to fulfill the purpose for which they were created, it would be necessary for them to objectively 'recover' that which was lost including life itself.

In the Old Testament the Hebrew for 'recover' is *qunah* which has several synonyms including 'purchase, ransom, attain, possess,' and most significantly, 'redeem.'

There is always a cost of/for redemption.

The remainder of the Bible from the closing of Genesis chapter 3 is the seamless scarlet thread describing the return to the presence of God and the recovery of life.

"So the LORD God banished him from the Garden of Eden to work the ground from which he had been taken. After he drove the man out, he placed on the east side of the Garden of Eden cherubim and a flaming sword...to guard the way to the tree of life." Genesis 3:23-24 NIV

Understanding redemption

Throughout the Bible God uses use His attributes to enact His redemptive plan. Such immutable attributes include His righteousness, justice, and love.

The Bible teaches that grace isn't free. Someone must pay for sin, and every sin must be reckoned with in God's time.

Redemption is illustrated in great detail in the Old Testament, and it is a Biblical fact that redemption for Adam and Eve and their descendants, including the nation of Israel and representatives of all other nations including the present age church, will be fulfilled in terms of Jewish law.

The doctrine of redemption was spelled out originally in the Levitical law. Another Hebrew word that was introduced for additional clarity of 'redemption' was *shuv* meaning 'to come back,' i.e. movement back to the point of departure.

Redemption explained with Levitical law

Now it can be seen that Adam and Eve's descendants, in order to return to the point of departure from God's presence due to disobedience, had to be purchased, or redeemed.

A significant aspect of Old Testament redemptive laws was the recovery of property or possessions which had been sold by a family member due to hardship.

"If one of your countrymen becomes poor and sells some of his property, his nearest relative is to come and redeem what his countryman has sold." Leviticus 25:25 NIV

The Levitical law also had provisions for the restoration of a family name if a husband died without a son to carry on the name. The deceased's wife could marry her husband's unmarried brother and their firstborn would bear the deceased's name. The applicable law was termed a Levirate marriage.

"If brothers are living together and one of them dies without a son, his widow must not marry outside the family. Her husband's brother shall take her and marry her and

fulfill the duty of a brother-in-law to her. The first son she bears shall carry on the name of the dead brother so that his name will not be blotted out from Israel." Deuteronomy 25:5-6 NIV

The combination of the law of redemption of property and the Levirate marriage provision were/are critically important in understanding the odyssey of all mankind throughout history - past, present, and future.

Detailed illustration of redemption

A wonderful example of both aspects of redemption is found in the Old Testament book of Ruth.

The events recorded in Ruth took place shortly before the time of the kings and approximately five centuries after the law was given to Moses and the Israelites.

"In the days when the judges ruled, there was a famine in the land, and a man from Bethlehem in Judah, together with his wife and two sons, went to live for a while in the country of Moab." Ruth 1:1 NIV

As the historical story unfolds, a family from the town of Bethlehem of Judah journeyed to the east of the Jordan River to Moab to find relief from the famine in Israel. The family consisted of the husband, his wife, and their two sons.

"The man's name was Elimelech, his wife's name Naomi, and the names of his two sons were Mahlon and Kilion. They were Ephrathites from Bethlehem, Judah. And they went to Moab and lived there. Now Elimelech, Naomi's husband, died, and she was left with her two sons. They married Moabite women, one named Orpah and the other Ruth. After they had lived there about ten years, both Mahlon and Kilion also died, and Naomi was left without her two sons and her husband." Ruth 1:2-5 NIV

So Naomi lost her husband. Then her two sons married women of Moab and both of her sons subsequently died, leaving Naomi not only a widow but also childless, with the exception of her two daughters-in-law, Orpah and Ruth.

When the famine in Judah ended, Naomi was determined to return to her homeland. She suggested that her daughters-in-law remain in the land of their nativity, i.e. Moab. Orpah did remain in Moab, but Ruth wanted to stay with her mother-in-law. She spoke the following words to Naomi:

"But Ruth replied, 'Don't urge me to leave you. Where you go I will go, and where you stay I will stay. Your people will be my people and your God my God.'" Ruth 1:16 NIV

Naomi quickly realized it was no use to try to talk Ruth out of her decision.

"When Naomi realized that Ruth was determined to go with her, she stopped urging her." Ruth 1:18 NIV

Thus Naomi and Ruth journeyed to Judah together.

"So Naomi returned from Moab accompanied by Ruth the Moabitess, her daughter-in-law, arriving in Bethlehem as the barley harvest was beginning." Ruth 1:22 NIV

Upon their return Naomi proclaimed to the women of the city of Bethlehem that God had inflicted hardship on her. She had sold, or was about to sell, a parcel of her deceased husband's land to alleviate her impoverished condition.

"I went away full, but the LORD has brought me back empty. Why call me Naomi? The LORD has afflicted me; the Almighty has brought misfortune upon me." Ruth 1:21 NIV

The name 'Naomi' means 'delight' or 'pleasant.'

Naomi had no idea how wonderfully God was using her in His divine eternal plan for mankind.

As Naomi and Ruth settled in, Ruth volunteered to glean barley to support herself and her mother-in-law. She would seek a landowner that would allow her to do so.

"And Ruth the Moabitess said to Naomi, 'Let me go to the fields and pick up the leftover grain behind anyone in whose eyes I find favor.' Naomi said to her, 'Go ahead, my daughter.'" Ruth 2:2 NIV

Ruth did providentially find such a field and landowner. At this time Ruth was unaware of the landowner's background and significance.

'*Then she left, and went and gleaned in the field after the reapers. And she happened to come to the part of the field belonging to Boaz, who was of the family of Elimelech.*" Ruth 2:3 NKJV

Note in the above the word 'happened' or 'hap' from the Hebrew *miqreh* has multiple synonyms including 'chance,' 'befall,' or 'accident.' However, *miqreh* is derived from *quarah* which means 'to bring about,' or 'appoint.'

In other words, God's plan was unfolding providentially and miraculously.

Boaz had immediately observed that Ruth was a virtuous woman.

"*Boaz replied, 'I've been told all about what you have done for your mother-in-law since the death of your husband – how you left your father and mother and your homeland and came to live with a people you did not know before.'*" Ruth 2:11 NIV

At the end of a day of gleaning, coupled with Boaz's kindness and generosity, Ruth returned to the city and her mother-in-law Naomi. Naomi was pleased with Ruth's bounty and inquired of where she had gleaned and for whom.

"*Her mother-in-law asked her, 'Where did you glean today? Where did you work? Blessed be the man who took notice of you!' Then Ruth told her mother-in-law about the one at whose place she had been working. 'The name of the man I worked with today is Boaz,' she said. 'The LORD bless him!' Naomi said to her daughter-in-law. 'He has not stopped showing his kindness to the living and the dead.' She added, 'That man is our close relative; he is one of our kinsman-redeemers.'"* Ruth 2:19-20 NIV

Three required components of redemption

Needless to say, Naomi immediately recognized and acknowledged God's hand in the situation. Her thoughts focused on the Jewish law of redemption. She reviewed in her mind the three components of Jewish redemptive law.

1) A lost possession

2) A willing close relative redeemer

3) A redemptive price

Now even though Boaz was willing to fulfill the role of redeemer, he knew there was one who was a closer relative to the deceased husband of Naomi than himself.

"Although it is true that I am near of kin, there is a kinsman-redeemer nearer than I." Ruth 3:12 NIV

The next step was for Boaz to explain the redemptive opportunity to the closer relative.

"Meanwhile Boaz went up to the town gate and sat there. When the Kinsman-redeemer he had mentioned came along, Boaz said, 'Come over here, my friend, and sit down.' So he went over and sat down. Boaz took ten of the elders of the town and said, 'Sit here,' and they did so. Then he said to the kinsman-redeemer, 'Naomi, who has come back from Moab, is selling the piece of land that belonged to our brother Elimelech. I thought I should bring the matter to your attention and suggest that you buy it in the presence of these seated here and in the presence of the elders of my people.'" Ruth 4:1-4a NIV

The relative initially said that he would in fact redeem the land in accordance with the Jewish law of redemption.

"'I will redeem it,' he said." Ruth 4:4b NIV

Then Boaz told the close relative that he must also perform the Levirate marriage provision of the law.

"Then Boaz said, 'On the day you buy the land from Naomi and from Ruth the Moabitess, you acquire the dead man's widow, in order to maintain the name of the dead with his property.'" Ruth 4:5 NIV

The close relative at this point declined, inasmuch as such a transaction would jeopardize his existing inheritance.

"At this, the kinsman-redeemer said, 'Then I cannot redeem it because I might endanger my own estate. You redeem it yourself. I cannot do it.'" Ruth 4:6 NIV

Thereupon Boaz announced that he would both redeem the lost possession as well as fulfill the Levirate marriage requirement.

"Then Boaz announced to the elders and all the people, 'Today you are witnesses that I have bought from Naomi all the property of Elimelech, Kilion and Mahlon. I have also acquired Ruth the Moabitess, Mahlon's widow, as my wife, in order to maintain the name of the dead with his property, so that his name will not disappear from among his family or from the town records. Today you are witnesses!'" Ruth 4:9-10 NIV

Then all the people and the elders of the city of Bethlehem were delighted.

"Then the elders and all those at the gate said, 'We are witnesses. May the LORD make the woman who is coming into your home like Rachel and Leah, who together built up the house of Israel. May you have standing in Ephrathah and be famous in Bethlehem. Through the offspring the LORD gives you by this young woman, may your family be like that of Perez, whom Tamar bore to Judah.'" Ruth 4:11-12 NIV

From Judah to David, the seed continues

Ruth did in fact conceive and bear a son.

"So Boaz took Ruth and she became his wife. Then he went to her, and the LORD enabled her to conceive, and she gave birth to a son. The women said to Naomi...'Praise be to the LORD, who this day has not left you without a kinsman-redeemer. May he become famous throughout Israel!'" Ruth 4:13-14 NIV

Note the wording, "the LORD enabled her to conceive." Their son would be named Obed and would be the grandfather of the future King David, and all were direct descendants of Judah.

"This, then, is the family line of Perez: Perez was the father of Hezron, Hezron the father of Ram, Ram the father of Amminadab, Amminadab the father of Nahshon, Nahshon the father of Salmon, Salmon the father of Boaz, Boaz the father of Obed, Obed the father of Jesse, and Jesse the father of David." Ruth 4:18-22 NIV

The significance of the events in the story of Ruth can be seen by examining the lineage of Jesus Christ, the ultimate Seed of the woman, and mankind's Redeemer.

"A record of the genealogy of Jesus Christ the son of David, the son of Abraham: Abraham was the father of Isaac, Isaac the father of Jacob, Jacob the father of Judah..." Matthew 1:1-2 NIV

God's promise to David

Three generations after the events recorded in the book of Ruth, God made a promise to Boaz's great grandson David while he ruled over the nation of Israel.

"When your days are over and you rest with your fathers, I will raise up your offspring (seed) to succeed you, who will come from your own body, and I will establish his kingdom. He is the one who will build a house for my Name, and I will establish the throne of his kingdom forever." 2 Samuel 7:12-13 NIV

David's son Solomon and his descendants would fulfill that part of the above prophecy, relative to building the temple and the right to rule the future kingdom.

"Salmon the father of Boaz, whose mother was Rahab, Boaz the father of Obed, whose mother was Ruth, Obed the father of Jesse, and Jesse the father of King David. David was the father of Solomon, whose mother had been Uriah's wife,... and Jacob the father of Joseph, the husband of Mary, of whom was born Jesus, who is called Christ." Matthew 1:5-6, 16 NIV

The promise God made to King David also included a 'Seed' to reign over an everlasting kingdom.

"Your house and your kingdom will endure forever before me; your throne will be established forever." 2 Samuel 7:16 NIV

This part of the promise was fulfilled in the genealogy of Mary the mother of Jesus.

"...the son of Melea, the son of Menna, the son of Mattatha, the son of Nathan, the son of David, the son of Jesse, the son of Obed, the son of Boaz, the son of Salmon, the son of Nashon..." Luke 3:31-32 NIV

Therefore, Luke provides the genealogy of Christ through Mary. Recall the Redeemer would be 'the Seed of the woman' from Genesis 3:15. No seed of man would be in Christ.

The genealogy given in Matthew is that of Joseph, the adoptive father of Jesus. That genealogy gave Christ the right to be the sovereign ruler of Israel, but not the blood line.

Thus it is seen that David's son Solomon was given the right to rule the future kingdom, while David's son Nathan provided the actual blood line for the 'Seed.'

There will be much more detail on the genealogy of Christ in chapter 8 entitled: ***The Kinsman Redeemer.***

The doctrine and application of redemption is found throughout history and recorded throughout the Bible beginning in Genesis and culminating in the final book of Revelation.

Chapter 5

What was the Lost Possession?

To better comprehend the doctrine of 'redemption' we need to know the full extent of the lost possession, i.e. what it is that needs to be redeemed.

When God created Adam and his counterpart in His own image, He blessed them and explained to them their God-given authority. Note in the following verse the fact that God talked or communicated with them, confirming their having been created in God's image.

"God blessed them and said to them, 'Be fruitful and increase in number; fill the earth and subdue it. Rule over the fish of the sea and the birds of the air and over every living creature that moves on the ground.'" Genesis 1:28 NIV

The Hebrew for the verb 'blessed' means 'an act of adoration by God to man,' with accompanying adverbs 'greatly' and 'abundantly.' It is the same word used when God called Abram (Abraham) and promised to make him a great nation.

"The LORD had said to Abram, 'Leave your country, your people and your father's household and go to the land I will show you. I will make you into a great nation and I will bless you...and all peoples on earth will be blessed through you.'" Genesis 12:1-3 NIV

The noun form of 'bless,' i.e. 'blessing' means 'benefit,' 'favor,' and/or a 'gift.'

From blessings to curse

After Eve was deceived and Adam disobeyed, God cursed the deceiver, along with Adam and his wife.

"So the LORD God said to the serpent, 'Because you have done this, cursed are you above all the livestock and all the wild animals!'" Genesis 3:14 NIV

The term 'cursed' in this verse means 'to bind with a spell,' 'to hem in with obstacles,' 'to render powerless.' It further limits the one being cursed from fulfilling their purpose without great difficulty.

The word has a different meaning when applied to a curse given by man.

Again, consider God's promise to Abraham.

"...and whoever curses you I will curse..." Genesis 12:3 NIV

Man's power to curse another is very much limited when compared with God's curse. The meaning of 'curse' above in the phrase 'him who curses you' means 'to consider one to be insignificant or of small worth; to be despised.'

In the last book of the Bible, the Greek meaning of the word blessed means 'to have the favor of God,' 'commendation,' 'one indwelt by the Spirit of God and/or marked by the fullness of God.'

"Blessed are those who wash their robes, that they may have the right to the tree of life and may go through the gates into the city." Revelation 22:14 NIV

That is a blessing that only God Himself can bestow.

The antonym for 'blessing' is as would be expected 'curse.'

"No longer will there be any curse. The throne of God and of the Lamb will be in the city..." Revelation 22:3 NIV

The Greek for 'curse' in the above verse is much stronger than 'anathema,' which means 'punishment for the sake of discipline;' it gives one over to divine condemnation; one devoted to destruction.

Therefore, the curse invoked by God on Adam and Eve and the Serpent in Genesis chapter 3 can only be removed by God. Likewise, the blessing spoken of in the final chapter of the Bible can only be given by God. Man is totally dependant on God's mercy and justice.

The consequences of not obeying the law

To lightly esteem or disobey the law in the Old Testament had deadly consequences.

"Cursed is the one who does not confirm all the words of this law." Deuteronomy 27:26 NKJV

No man in any time in history could fulfill God's standard of righteousness and justice.

"All who rely on observing the law are under a curse, for it is written: 'Cursed is everyone who does not continue to do everything written in the Book of the Law.'" Galatians 3:10 NIV

Therefore, all under the law required redemption.

Removing the curse

Let's examine firstly the broader significance of the curse pronounced in Genesis.

Adam and Eve were expelled from the garden, i.e. they were no longer in the direct presence of God. They were denied access to the tree of life, which meant they would die. Their offspring would no longer be born with the Spirit of God within them.

In other words, their descendants would be conceived and born into sin. They were rendered powerless and lost their privilege of dominion over all other living things on the earth, which was also subject to the curse.

The life that Adam and Eve lost had included 'living forever' and, interestingly, in the Hebrew life included 'fresh, running water.' Death is the direct opposite of life.

They had lost everything!

The first mention of the term 'redemption' found in the Bible is in the latter part of Genesis and spoken by Jacob to his son Joseph.

"The Angel who has redeemed me from all evil, bless the lads; let my name be named upon them, and the name of my fathers Abraham and Isaac; and let them grow into a multitude in the midst of the earth." Genesis 48:16 NKJV

As Jacob was pronouncing blessings on Joseph's sons Ephraim and Manasseh, he acknowledged that 'the Angel,' i.e. Angel of the LORD or God Himself, had redeemed him from all evil.

As previously stated, the Hebrew for 'redeemed' means 'to purchase, pay a ransom, or to deliver.' Another interesting synonym is 'kinsman,' inasmuch as according to Jewish law, a kinsman, or close relative, was required to consummate the redemption process.

Redemption became a major doctrine in Israel's odyssey

Moses stressed the importance of obeying God's laws in full. The Israelites were to study and meditate on the law at all times and diligently teach the law to their children. They could not pick and choose which parts of the law to obey.

"These commandments that I give you today are to be upon your hearts. Impress them on your children. Talk about them when you sit at home and when you walk along the road, when you lie down and when you get up. Tie them as symbols on your hands and bind them on your foreheads. Write them on the doorframes of your houses and on your gates." Deuteronomy 6:6-9 NIV

And when Moses confirmed to the Israelites that they were God's chosen people, a treasure above all other peoples on the face of the earth, he reminded them that God had 'brought you out' or delivered them from Egyptian bondage.

"...the LORD...brought you out with a mighty hand and redeemed you from the land of slavery, from the power of Pharaoh king of Egypt." Deuteronomy 7:8 NIV

The specific Hebrew term for 'redeemed' in this verse is *padhah* which means, in addition to the equivalent synonyms listed above, 'to set free from servitude.'

The doctrine of redemption is found throughout the Old Testament relative to God's chosen people, i.e. the descendants of Abraham, Isaac, and Jacob.

Approximately half millennia after the law was given, the Psalmist spoke of Israel's future redemption.

"O Israel, put your hope in the LORD, for with the LORD is unfailing love and with him is full redemption. He himself will redeem Israel from all their sins." Psalm 130:7-8 NIV

And while God had redeemed Israel from Egyptian oppression, they had sinned repeatedly and would require redemption from the bondage of sin.

"Remember these things, O Jacob, for you are my servant, O Israel. I have made you...O Israel, I will not forget you. I have swept away your offenses like a cloud, your sins like the morning mist. Return to me, for I have redeemed you." Isaiah 44:21-22 NIV

The Prophet Micah addressed that very issue. As Israel continued in sin and rebellion, God reminded them of what He had done on their behalf. He was tender in pleading His case against them.

"My people, what have I done to you? How have I burdened you? Answer me. I brought you up out of Egypt and redeemed you from the land of slavery..." Micah 6:3-4 NIV

Israel's future was/is totally in the hands of their sovereign God. Redemption was their only hope.

Universal aspects of redemption

Redemption covers more than just national Israel and mankind. Recall that the curse invoked by God involved the physical earth.

"...Cursed is the ground because of you; through painful toil you will eat of it all the days of your life. It will produce thorns and thistles for you, and you will eat the plants of the field. By the sweat of your brow you will eat your food until you return to the ground, since from it you were taken..." Genesis 3:17b-19 NIV

Adam and his descendants would be required to labor and sweat in order for the earth to be productive. And so it is to this day.

Paul also addressed the universal curse in his writings to the Christians in Rome.

"For the creation was subject to futility, not willingly; but because of Him who subjected it in hope..." Romans 8:20 NKJV

The Greek for 'subject' means 'to subjugate, or place in submission' while the word 'futility' means 'vanity, emptiness, fruitless, or aimless.' In this present age, man is impotent to fulfill God's purpose and plan. Sin has a profound effect.

But Paul looks forward to universal deliverance.

"...because the creation itself also will be delivered from the bondage of corruption into the glorious liberty of the children of God." Romans 8:21 NKJV

Inasmuch as the whole creation was/is affected by man's sin, redemption will remove all affects of the curse. Recall the broad meaning of the word 'deliver.' 'Deliver' not only means 'redemption,' but other synonyms include 'free' resulting from a ransom payment, 'reconciliation,' and 'propitiation.'

In other words, the universal curse will be removed with universal redemption.

The term 'bondage' in the above verse means 'slavery' or 'servitude.' Such is in direct contrast with sonship.

The term 'corruption' in the above verse means 'mortal, subject to decay or deterioration.'

In summary, redemption is required to restore mankind and the earth to their pre-curse freedom.

However, as history unfolds, it will become clear that the majority of mankind will reject God's redemptive plan.

Chapter 6

The Bible's Scarlet Thread

The Hebrew word 'thread' means 'twine or bind together.' And 'scarlet' does in fact mean color, i.e. crimson or red. The Bible's scarlet thread that binds all Scripture together is the blood.

The Hebrew word for 'blood' in the Old Testament is *dam*. There are two major issues concerning blood in the Old Testament, i.e. the shedding of the blood of innocent man and the shedding of blood of an animal while making a sacrifice to God. Both result in death of the one whose blood is shed.

Interestingly, *dam* is also used metaphorically to represent red wine, or the juice of grapes.

Blood and life

Blood is the essence of life; therefore, to lose blood is to lose life itself. One of the most significant Scripture passages in the Bible is found in Leviticus.

"For the life of the flesh is in the blood, and I have given it to you upon the altar to make atonement for your souls; for it is the blood that makes atonement for the soul...for it (blood) is the life of all flesh. Its (living thing) blood sustains its life..." Leviticus 17:11, 14a NKJV

'Life' in this passage is from the Hebrew *nephesh* meaning 'a breathing creature, animal or man.'

Man was created from the dust of the earth and was made a living being in the image of his Creator. Man in his initial state consisted of flesh and bones. The Hebrew word for 'flesh' means 'mortal body,' or the 'external aspect of man.' 'Bones' represent 'the frame of the mortal body.' Blood flowed through the flesh to sustain the life of a mortal body.

And while Adam was created from the dust, his counterpart Eve was called woman made from the bone of Adam.

"The man said, 'This is now bone of my bones and flesh of my flesh; she shall be called 'woman,' for she was taken out of man.'" Genesis 2:23 NIV

As God revealed His timeless plan for man He provided blood of animals to temporarily cover the sins of man. Recall the significant passage describing Adam and Eve's covering when they were driven out from the Garden of Eden.

"The LORD God made garments of skin for Adam and his wife and clothed them." Genesis 3:21 NIV

'God made' and 'God clothed.' Adam and Eve's self-made covering of leaves was not sufficient to cover their sin of disobedience. Their sin could only be atoned for with blood, confirming the loss or sacrifice of a life.

The same truth was the center of the controversy between the brothers Cain and Abel. In fact, the first mention of the word 'blood' in the Bible is found in the story of these two brothers.

"The LORD said, 'What have you done? Listen! Your brother's blood cries out to me from the ground. Now you are under a curse and driven from the ground, which opened its mouth to receive your brother's blood from your hand.'" Genesis 4:10-11 NIV

After the flood judgment, God told Noah that every living animal, bird, or fish could be food for him and his family. He did, however, make one very significant restriction.

"But you must not eat meat that has its lifeblood still in it." Genesis 9:4 NIV

Also at that time God made it a capital offense to kill, i.e. murder an innocent human.

"...And from each man, too, I will demand an accounting for the life of his fellow man. 'Whoever sheds the blood of

man, by man shall his blood be shed; for in the image of God has God made man.'" Genesis 9:5b-6 NIV

The Passover

Recall God told Jacob not to be afraid to go down to Egypt because God had a plan for his family. They would become a great nation during their servitude.

"...Do not be afraid to go down to Egypt, for I will make you into a great nation there. I will go down to Egypt with you, and I will surely bring you back again." Genesis 46:3-4 NIV

The term 'go down with...you' meant that God would humble them and the term 'bring you back' meant that God would exalt them.

God was confirming His promise made to Jacob's grandfather Abraham. The phrase 'surely bring you up again' meant that God would without a doubt 'exalt' Israel as promised by delivering them out of Egyptian bondage.

Four hundred years later God confirmed to Moses His promise to redeem Israel.

"...and I will bring you out from under the yoke of the Egyptians. I will free you from being slaves to them, and I will redeem you with an outstretched arm...I will take you as my own people, and I will be your God...and I will bring you to the land I swore with uplifted hand to give to

Abraham, to Isaac and to Jacob. I will give it to you as a possession." Exodus 6:6-8 NIV

God's plan for deliverance, or redemption, would be introduced and illustrated with the 'Passover.' This plan was revealed immediately prior to Israel's deliverance.

"Now the LORD spoke to Moses...saying, 'This month shall be your beginning of months; it shall be the first month of the year to you...On the tenth of this month every man shall take for himself a lamb...your lamb shall be without blemish...Now you shall keep it until the fourteenth day of the same month. Then the whole assembly of the congregation of Israel shall kill it at twilight. And they shall take some of the blood and put it on the two doorposts and on the lintel of the houses where they eat it.'" Exodus 12:1-3, 5-7 NKJV

The Hebrew word for 'twilight' means 'between evenings.' According to the Jewish historian Josephus, the killing of the paschal lamb was customarily done at 3:00 PM.

The lamb chosen was to be without blemish (defect). It was to be kept for four days and then slain. A further requirement was that not a bone of the lamb should be broken.

"...do not break any of the bones." Exodus 12:46b NIV

The blood of the lamb was to be sprinkled on both sides of the door, as well as on the top of the door of the houses.

"The blood will be a sign for you on the houses where you are; and when I see the blood, I will pass over you. No destructive plague will touch you when I strike Egypt. This is a day you are to commemorate; for the generations to come you shall celebrate it as a festival to the LORD – a lasting ordinance." Exodus 12:13-14 NIV

Shortly thereafter the deliverance of the Israelites would be termed their 'redemption.' After their deliverance when Moses was explaining the reasoning relative to God's love for Israel as His chosen nation, he said:

"But it was because the LORD loved you and kept the oath he swore to your forefathers that he brought you out with a mighty hand and redeemed you from the land of slavery, from the power of Pharaoh king of Egypt." Deuteronomy 7:8 NIV

Worship through offerings

Shortly after the Exodus, God began to reveal His prescribed methods of worship required of the Israelites. In the present context the focus will be on several specific offerings including burnt offerings, sin offerings, and trespass offerings.

The burnt offering was a voluntary offering; however, there were specific details required. God spoke to Moses from the tabernacle of meeting and provided specific instructions.

"If his offering is a burnt sacrifice of the herd, let him offer a male without blemish; he shall offer it of his own free will at the door of the tabernacle...Then he shall put his hand on the head of the burnt offering; and it will be accepted on his behalf to make atonement for him. He shall kill the bull...and Aaron's sons, shall bring the blood and sprinkle the blood all around on the altar." Leviticus 1:2-5 NKJV

Firstly, the offering was to be a male without blemish (defect) and was to be offered of one's own free will. The one presenting the offering was to put his hand on the head of the burnt offering, symbolizing the transfer of sins to the animal.

Blood was first drained, presented to the LORD, and then sprinkled on the altar. The offering was then to be completely burned up, making a 'sweet aroma to the LORD.'

Sin and trespass offerings

The sin offering and trespass (guilt) offering were closely related.

"The same law applies to both the sin offering and the guilt (trespass) offering..." Leviticus 7:7 NIV

Both the sin offering and trespass offering were compulsory and atoned for sins committed unknowingly, or unintentionally. One difference, however, was that restitution was possible for a transgression classified as a trespass, while not possible for a transgression requiring a sin offering.

Intentional, or highhanded, sins were handled differently.

"But anyone who sins defiantly, whether native-born or alien, blasphemes the LORD, and that person must be cut off (killed) from his people." Numbers 15:30 NIV

Detailed requirements of the sin offering included offering a young bull without blemish.

"He is to present the bull at the entrance to the Tent of Meeting before the LORD. He is to lay his hand on its head and slaughter it before the LORD... He is to dip his finger into the blood and sprinkle some of it seven times before the LORD, in front of the curtain of the sanctuary. The priest shall then put some of the blood on the horns of the altar of fragrant incense...The rest of the bull's blood he shall pour out at the base of the altar of burnt offering..." Leviticus 4:4-7 NIV

Again, the one bringing the offering would lay his hand on the head of the offering, and kill it. Blood of the offering was sprinkled in front of the veil of the most holy place, some was placed on the horns of the altar of incense, and the rest was poured out at the base of the altar of burnt offering.

The annual Day of Atonement

The 'Day of Atonement' was observed once each year. This hallowed day was appointed on the tenth day of the seventh month. The purpose was to atone for Aaron the High Priest, the entire priesthood, Aaron's family, all the Israelites, and the tabernacle itself.

There were very specific instructions provided by God for the Day of Atonement.

The Hebrew word for 'atonement' is *kaphar* with multiple meaning; however, its primary meaning is 'to cover.' It also means 'to placate, appease, pacify,' and to 'put off.'

"This is to be a lasting ordinance for you: Atonement is to be made once a year for all the sins of the Israelites." Leviticus 16:34 NIV

God told Moses that Aaron was to enter the Holy place only on the Day of Atonement.

And before entering the Holy place Aaron was to remove his high priestly attire which included a breastplate, an ephod, a robe, a skillfully woven tunic, a turban, and a sash. He was to wash his body in water and put on normal priestly attire which included a linen tunic and linen trousers. He was to be girded with a linen sash.

"Thus Aaron shall come into the Holy Place: with the blood of a young bull as a sin offering, and of a ram as a

burnt offering...Aaron shall offer the bull as a sin offering, which is for himself, and make atonement for himself and for his house...inside the veil...He shall take some of the blood of the bull and sprinkle it with his finger on the mercy seat...and before the mercy seat he shall sprinkle some of the blood with his finger seven times." Leviticus 16:3, 6, 14 NKJV

After making atonement for himself and his family, he was to make atonement for all the children of Israel.

"And he (Aaron) shall take from the congregation of the children of Israel two kids of the goats as a sin offering, and one ram as a burnt offering." Leviticus 16:5 NKJV

One of the goats was to be killed and its blood offered, while the other goat was to be let go in the wilderness representing the removal of the sins of the children of Israel.

"He (Aaron) shall take the two goats and...cast lots for the two goats: one lot for the LORD and the other lot for the scapegoat. And Aaron shall bring the goat on which the LORD's lot fell, and offer it as a sin offering." Leviticus 16:7-9 NKJV

Aaron was to reenter the Holy place with the blood of the sin offering for the people, just as he had offered the blood of his own sin offering.

"Then he (Aaron) shall kill the goat of the sin offering, which is for the people, bring its blood inside the veil, do

with that blood as he did with the blood of the bull, and sprinkle it on the mercy seat and before the mercy seat." Leviticus 16:15 NKJV

This sin offering also atoned for the Holy place itself.

"So he shall make atonement for the Holy Place, because of the uncleanness of the children of Israel, and because of their transgressions, for all their sins..." Leviticus 16:16 NKJV

Only Aaron was to be in the tabernacle when he entered the Holy place.

"There shall be no man in the tabernacle of meeting when he goes in to make atonement in the Holy Place... that he may make atonement for himself, for his household, and for all the assembly of Israel." Leviticus 16:17 NKJV

Then Aaron was to make atonement for the altar of burnt offering in the outer court of the tabernacle.

"And he shall go out to the altar that is before the LORD, and make atonement for it, and shall take some of the blood of the bull and some of the blood of the goat, and put it on the horns of the altar all around. Then he shall sprinkle some of the blood on it with his finger seven times, cleanse it, and consecrate it from the uncleanness of the children of Israel." Leviticus 16:18-19 NKJV

It's all about the blood!

After the atonement and blood offering, it was time to deal with the live goat.

"And when he has made an end of atoning for the Holy Place, the tabernacle of meeting, and the altar, he shall bring the live goat. Aaron shall lay both his hands on the head of the live goat, confess over it all the iniquities of the children of Israel...putting them on the head of the goat, and shall send it away into the wilderness...The goat shall bear on itself all their iniquities to an uninhabited land..." Leviticus 16:20-22 NKJV

Then Aaron would return to the tabernacle, remove his regular priestly garments, wash his body again with water, and put back on his High priestly garments.

"Then Aaron shall come into the tabernacle of meeting, shall take off the linen garments which he put on when he went into the Holy Place, and shall leave them there. And he shall wash his body with water in a holy place, put on his garments, come out and offer his burnt offering and the burnt offering of the people..." Leviticus 16:23-24 NKJV

The Day of Atonement is one of the seven original Levitical feasts. What a wonderful detailed picture of the significance of the blood for the atonement of sin. Remember, however, that 'atonement' means to 'cover' or 'put off.' It does not 'once for all' deal with sin.

God's meeting place with Moses

Specific instructions were given for the design and construction of the ark and mercy seat where God would communicate with Moses.

"And they (children of Israel) shall make an ark,....You shall make a mercy seat...You shall put the mercy seat on top of the ark, and in the ark you shall put the Testimony that I will give you. And there I will meet with you, and I will speak with you from above the mercy seat...about everything which I will give you in commandment to the children of Israel." Exodus 25:10, 17, 21-22 NKJV

And so it was:

"When Moses entered the Tent (tabernacle) of Meeting to speak with the LORD, he heard the voice speaking to him from between the two cherubim above the atonement cover (mercy seat). And he spoke with him." Numbers 7:89 NIV

The covenant between God and His chosen people

Prior to the construction of the Tabernacle, God called Moses to His presence and confirmed His standard of conduct for the people. Moses wrote all the words of the LORD in a book and subsequently relayed all of God's words to the people. The people accepted all of God's words, and the covenant was ratified with the blood of burnt offerings and peace offerings.

"Moses took half of the blood and put it in bowls, and the other half he sprinkled on the altar. Then he took the Book of the Covenant and read it to the people. They responded, 'We will do everything the LORD has said; we will obey.' Moses then took the blood, sprinkled it on the people and said, 'This is the blood of the covenant that the LORD has made with you in accordance with all these words.'"
Exodus 24:6-8 NIV

The Hebrew for 'covenant' means 'agreement,' and this covenant confirmed God's initial covenant with Abraham, along with subsequent revelations including the Ten Commandments. The Hebrew for 'sprinkled' symbolized an unbreakable bond between God and man.

The old was the model for the new

This very same covenant was referred to in the New Testament 1500 years later.

"When Moses had proclaimed every commandment of the law to all the people, he took the blood...and sprinkled the scroll and all the people. He said, 'This is the blood of the covenant, which God has commanded you to keep.' In the same way, he sprinkled with the blood both the tabernacle and everything used in its ceremonies." Hebrews 9:19-21 NIV

This chapter has thus far focused on the blood sacrifice, i.e. the offering of an animal to substitute for the human offender and the significance of the blood in ratifying a covenant.

How important is the blood sacrifice?

"...and without shedding of blood there is no remission." Hebrews 9:22 NKJV

The Greek word 'remission' has several synonyms, i.e. 'forgiveness, liberty, and deliverance.'

However, that great truth presents a problem for mankind, when the efficacy of Old Testament sacrificial offerings is considered.

"The law is only a shadow of the good things that are coming – not the realities themselves. For this reason it can never, by the same sacrifices repeated endlessly year after year, make perfect those who draw near to worship... because **it is impossible for the blood of bulls and goats to take away sins***."* Hebrews 10:1, 4 NIV (emphasis added)

Man has a problem!

Chapter 7

Man's Great Dilemma Solved

Without the shedding of blood, there was no remission of sins; however, the blood of animals was not sufficient payment for sins.

"...because it is impossible for the blood of bulls and goats to take away sins." Hebrews 10:4 NIV

Was the Book of the Covenant between God and His people that Moses ratified with the sprinkling of blood to no avail?

Fear not, God's master plan for His chosen was right on schedule. His purpose would not, could not fail.

"But when the time had fully come, God sent his Son, born of a woman, born under law, to redeem those under law..." Galatians 4:4-5 NIV

God's Son was the Seed of the woman promised by God to bruise Satan's head in the Garden of Eden.

"And I will put enmity between you and the woman, and between your seed and her Seed; He shall bruise your head, and you shall bruise His heel." Genesis 3:15 NKJV

Remember what Jesus said relative to the law on His famous sermon on the mount.

"Do not think that I have come to abolish (destroy) the Law or the Prophets; I have not come to abolish them but to fulfill them. I tell you the truth, until heaven and earth disappear, not the smallest letter, not the least stroke of a pen, will by any means disappear from the Law until everything is accomplished." Matthew 5:17-18 NIV

The Old Testament Passover Lamb is fulfilled in the New Testament

Recall when God instituted the Passover immediately before freeing the Israelites from Egyptian bondage. They were to eat the flesh of the lamb with unleavened bread. As they left Egypt they were to eat unleavened bread for seven days.

"In the first month, on the fourteenth day of the month at evening, you shall eat unleavened bread, until the twenty-first day of the month at evening. For seven days no leaven shall be found in your houses...you shall eat nothing leavened; in all your dwellings you shall eat unleavened bread." Exodus 12:18-20 NKJV

Unleavened bread was baked without yeast. Yeast was normally used to make the bread rise during baking and would affect the characteristics of the whole loaf. Unleavened bread was not fermented or made bitter with yeast. It also signified the haste with which the Israelites left Egypt.

The Passover lamb without leaven was indeed fulfilled in the New Testament.

"...Do you not know that a little leaven leavens the whole lump? Therefore purge out the old leaven, that you may be a new lump, since you truly are unleavened. For indeed Christ, our Passover, was sacrificed for us. Therefore let us keep the feast, not with old leaven, nor with the leaven of malice and wickedness, but with the unleavened bread of sincerity and truth." 1 Corinthians 5:6-8 NKJV

The Greek meaning of 'leaven' is similar to the Hebrew, i.e. it is an added ingredient to ferment or change the characteristic of something. When used in Scripture it generally signifies evil or wicked influence which will gradually overtake and corrupt the whole person. Jesus warned His disciples to beware of the leaven of the Pharisees. He meant for them to avoid the doctrine of the Pharisees.

Therefore, Christ as the Passover Lamb without blemish was to be embraced wholly without any external or worldly diluting influence.

Redemption in the New Testament

One of the major definitions of redemption in the New Testament is from the Greek *apolutrosis* which means in general 'to be delivered from the power and consequence of sin upon the payment of a ransom.'

"For he chose us in him before the creation (foundation) of the world...In him we have redemption through his blood, the forgiveness of sins..." Ephesians 1:4, 7 NIV

This passage confirms that God's plan to redeem mankind was designed before the earth ever was. He subsequently implemented that indescribable plan step by step and fulfilled it via His Son.

Paul preached the message of redemption to all the churches.

"For he has rescued us from the dominion of darkness and brought us into the kingdom of the Son he loves, in whom we have redemption, the forgiveness of sins...For God was pleased to have all his fullness dwell in him, and through him to reconcile to himself all things, whether things on earth or things in heaven, by making peace through his blood, shed on the cross." Colossians 1:13-14, 19-20 NIV

Christ was God in the flesh in accordance with the Father's delight and purpose. Christ reconciled all things, i.e. established a relationship of peace that heretofore could not exist while man remained in sin. Man's former state of enmity had been replaced with reconciliation. It was only possible by Christ, the perfect Lamb of God, shedding His blood as the ransom paid to deliver man from the bondage of sin.

The Passover lamb was a foreshadow of the Lamb of God who was revealed in this present age (last times) to fulfill the law of atonement exemplified by forfeiting life proven by the shedding of blood.

The writer of the Book of Hebrews summarized the issue perfectly. He first reviewed the Old Testament laws regarding offerings with the qualifier that such laws were symbolic (parabolic) for the present age. He then confirms the fulfillment of the Old Testament law by Christ.

"When Christ came as high priest of the good things that are already here...He did not enter by means of the blood of goats and calves; but he entered the Most Holy Place once for all by his own blood, having obtained eternal redemption...For this reason Christ is the mediator of a new covenant, that those who are called may receive the promised eternal inheritance..." Hebrews 9:11-12, 15 NIV

Christ's sacrifice was 'once for all' while sacrifices under the Old Testament law had to be made repeatedly. It was not until Christ's sacrifice that the sins of those called in the Old Testament were actually paid for, providing and guaranteeing the eternal inheritance.

Justification and propitiation

As Paul wrote to the Christians in Rome, his primary message was the work of Christ in fulfilling the Old Testament law.

"But now a righteousness from God, apart from law, has been made known...for all have sinned and fall short of the glory of God, and are justified freely by his grace through the redemption that came by Christ Jesus. God presented him as a sacrifice of atonement (propitiation), through faith in his blood...to demonstrate his justice, because in his forbearance he had left the sins committed beforehand unpunished..." Romans 3:21, 23-25 NIV

Paul confirmed that the law was just a tutor until Christ came to fulfill the law. He then told that all mankind had failed; however, 'justified' (a legal term meaning to be declared righteous) was offered freely by the vicarious death of Christ. The Greek word for 'propitiation' is *hilasterios* meaning 'mercy seat.' 'Propitiation' further means 'the propitiatory gift offered to God for His mercy.'

"He (Christ) is the atoning sacrifice (propitiation) for our sins, and not only for ours but also for the sins of the whole world." 1 John 2:2 NIV

"This is love; not that we loved God, but that he loved us and sent his Son as an atoning sacrifice (propitiation) for our sins." 1 John 4:10 NIV

Recall in the Old Testament the mercy seat was the covering of the Ark of the Covenant. The mercy seat was the place where God would speak to Moses. It was also the place where the high priest would sprinkle the blood of the sacrifices on the Day of Atonement. Paul was explaining that Christ was the true mercy seat or propitiation in the total sense of the word.

"The Holy Spirit was showing by this that the way into the Most Holy Place had not yet been disclosed as long as the first tabernacle was still standing. This is an illustration for the present time...When Christ came as high priest...He did not enter by means of the blood of goats and calves; but he entered the Most Holy Place once for all by his own blood, having obtained eternal redemption...For this reason Christ is the mediator of a new covenant, that those who are called may receive the promised eternal inheritance..." Hebrews 9:8-9a, 11-12, 15 NIV

The new covenant

Just as the Old Testament covenant was ratified with the blood of animal sacrifices, the new covenant is ratified with the blood of Christ.

While partaking of His final Passover meal, Jesus announced the new covenant. He took the cup of wine, blessed it, and told His disciples to drink of it.

"For this is My blood of the new covenant, which is shed for many for the remission (forgiveness) of sins." Matthew 26:28 NKJV

Paul repeated Jesus' words to the church at Corinth. The old covenant, which was a shadow of things to come, was replaced with the new and everlasting covenant. The church was to celebrate the 'Lord's supper' to remind them of the work on the cross.

"In the same way, after supper he took the cup, saying, 'This cup is the new covenant in my blood; do this, whenever you drink it, in remembrance of me.'" 1 Corinthians 11:25 NIV

The writer of Hebrews pronounced a stern warning for those who take lightly the blood of Christ and the new covenant.

"Anyone who rejected the law of Moses died without mercy...How much more severely do you think a man deserves to be punished who has trampled the Son of God under foot, who has treated as an unholy thing the blood of the covenant that sanctified him, and who has insulted the Spirit of Grace?" Hebrews 10:28-29 NIV

Chapter 8

The Kinsman Redeemer

It has been determined that Jesus Christ is indeed the 'Seed of the Woman,' but does He literally fulfill the requirement to be the kinsman redeemer in terms of the Jewish law? We've described the lost possession and the redemptive price; now we need to establish and confirm the third required component, i.e. a close relative to qualify as the Redeemer.

It all began with Adam and Eve. The lost possession was described as their life and the curse over the whole earth. They had lost access to the tree of life and they no longer could be in the presence of God.

Therefore, the kinsman redeemer must be related to Adam and Eve.

Adam and Eve began to procreate with two sons, Cain and Abel. Cain was called a son of the evil one while Abel was deemed righteous. Cain murdered his righteous brother Abel, which was the first attempt by Satan to prevent the

Seed of the woman and eliminate any possible redeemer to buy back the lost possession.

But Adam and Eve had a third son named Seth.

"Adam lay with his wife again, and she gave birth to a son and named him Seth, saying, 'God has granted me another child in place of Abel, since Cain killed him.'" Genesis 4:25 NIV

So the lineage of Adam and Eve needs to be examined to determine if one of their descendants meets the qualification of kinsman redeemer.

See **figure 4-1**

Adam and Eve's Descendants from Seth to Shem

Adam begot Seth when 130 years old	Genesis 5:3	Luke 3:38
Seth begot Enosh when 105 years old	Genesis 5:6	Luke 3:38
Enosh begot Cainan when 90 years old	Genesis 5:9	Luke 3:37
Cainan begot Mahalalel when 70 years old	Genesis 5:12	Luke 3:37
Mahalalel begot Jared when 65 years old	Genesis 5:15	Luke 3:37
Jared begot Enoch when 162 years old	Genesis 5:18	Luke 3:37
Enoch begot Methuselah when 65 years old	Genesis 5:21	Luke 3:37
Methuselah begot Lamech when 187 years old	Genesis 5:25	Luke 3:36
Lamech begot Noah when 182 years old	Genesis 5:28-29	Luke 3:36
Noah begot Shem, Ham, and Japeth when 500 years old*	Genesis 5:32	Luke 3:36

* Noah's three sons are listed together so it cannot be determined with certainty which son was his first born.

Figure 4-1 Family tree of Adam and Eve up to and including Noah's son Shem.

It is also significant to note that when Noah was born his father Lamech commented:

"He will comfort us in the labor and painful toil of our hands caused by the ground the LORD has cursed." Genesis 5:29 NIV

Adam and Eve's Lineage from Shem to Abram (Abraham)

Shem begot Arphaxad when 100 years old	Genesis 11:10	Luke 3:36
Arphaxad begot Salah when 35 years old	Genesis 11:12	Luke 3:36
Salah begot Eber when 30 years old	Genesis 11:14	Luke 3:35
Eber begot Peleg when 34 years old	Genesis 11:16	Luke 3:35
Peleg begot Reu when 30 years old	Genesis 11:18	Luke 3:35
Reu begot Serug when 32 years old	Genesis 11:20	Luke 3:35
Serug begot Nahor when 30 years old	Genesis 11:22	Luke 3:34
Nahor begot Terah when 29 years old	Genesis 11:24	Luke 3:34
Terah begot Abram when 70 years old *	Genesis 11:26	Luke 3:34

Figure 4-2 Family tree from Noah's son Shem to Abram

* Again the Bible lists Terah's sons Abram, Nahor, and Haran together, thus making it uncertain which son was born first.

However, an approximate time period between Adam and Abram can be determined by considering that Seth was the firstborn of Adam's sons after Cain and Abel and likewise that Abram was the firstborn of Terah.

The total elapsed time between Adam and Abram is approximately 1946 years, and when added to the approximate year of Abram's birth, i.e. 2165 BC would place the creation of Adam at approximately 4111 BC.

"A record of the genealogy of Jesus Christ the son of David, the son of Abraham: ..." Matthew 1:1 NIV

Abraham begot Isaac
Isaac begot Jacob
Jacob begot Judah
Judah begot Perez
Perez begot Hezron
Hezron begot Ram
Ram begot Amminadab
Amminadab begot Nashon
Nashon begot Salmon
Salmon begot Boaz
Boaz begot Obed
Obed begot Jesse
Jesse begot David the king

Figure 4-3 Family tree from Abram (Abraham) to David

The lineage from Abraham to King David is exactly the same as recorded in Matthew 1:2-6 and Luke 3:31-34.

It was while David was king that God provided more details of His plan, initially revealed to Abraham.

"When your days are over and you rest with your fathers, I will raise up your offspring (seed) to succeed you, who will come from your own body, and I will establish his kingdom. He is the one who will build a house for my Name, and I will establish the throne of his kingdom forever." 2 Samuel 7:12-13 NIV

These revealing and profound verses contain three of God's famous 'I will' promises.

The Hebrew meaning of 'house' in the above means 'family' or 'descendant' while the Hebrew meaning for 'throne' means basically 'the right to reign.' 'House' can also mean 'a physical temple.' 'Kingdom' is likewise a synonym of 'reign.'

Thus David is told that the seed of his own body will reign over a kingdom that God will establish forever. The seed of his body would also build a temple for God's name.

Now as the genealogy of Christ is examined, it is noted that from David to Christ, according to Matthew, is not the same as from David to Christ, according to Luke.

According to Matthew:

David begot Solomon
Solomon begot Rehoboam
Rehoboam begot Abijah
Abijah begot Asa
Asa Begot Jehoshaphat
Jehoshaphat begot Jehoram
Jehoram begot Uzziah
Uzziah begot Jotham
Jotham begot Ahaz
Ahaz begot Hezekiah
Hezekiah begot Manasseh
Manasseh begot Amon

Amon begot Josiah
Josiah begot Jeconiah
Jeconiah begot Shealtiel
Shealtiel begot Zerubbabel
Zerubbabel begot Abiud
Abiud begot Eliakim
Eliakim begot Azor
Azor begot Zadok
Zadok begot Achim
Achim begot Eliud
Eliud begot Eleazar
Eleazar begot Matthan
Matthan begot Jacob
Jacob begot Joseph the husband of Mary, of whom was born
Jesus who is called Christ.

Firstly, it is noted that while the above is totally correct,
it does not include each successive step in the family; i.e.
Josiah had several sons that ruled Judah for very short
times, including Jehoahaz, Jehoiakim and Zedekiah. These
three ruled just prior to the time Judah was deported to
Babylon.

Josiah's son Jeconiah, (also referred to as Jehoiachin or
Coniah) did evil in the sight of the LORD and reigned for
just three months and 10 days.

*"This is what the LORD says: 'Go down to the palace
of the king of Judah and proclaim this message there: Hear
the word of the LORD, O king of Judah, you who sit on*

David's throne – you, your officials and your people who come through these gates...Record this man (Jeconiah/ Coniah) as if childless, a man who will not prosper in his lifetime, for none of his offspring will prosper, none will sit on the throne of David or rule anymore in Judah.'"
Jeremiah 22:1, 30 NIV

So Jeremiah was told to advise Coniah that he would never have a seed to sit on the throne of David. That being the case, how did that affect the promise made to David that his seed would sit on the throne forever?

The answer is that while Coniah is in the messianic lineage according to Matthew, the lineage ends with Joseph, the adoptive father of Jesus. The right to rule was given, but not the seed, i.e. the Seed of the woman.

We need to refer to the lineage of Christ given in Luke.

Note that this lineage is different, beginning with David's sons Nathan and Solomon.

David begot Nathan
Nathan begot Mattathah
Mattathah begot Menan
Menan begot Melea
Melea begot Eliakim
Eliakim begot Jonan
Jonan begot Joseph
Joseph begot Judah
Judah begot Simeon

Simeon begot Levi

Levi begot Matthat

Matthat begot Jorim

Jorim begot Eliezer

Eliezer begot Jose

Jose begot Er

Er begot Elmodam

Elmodam begot Cosam

Cosam begot Addi

Addi begot Melchi

Melchi begot Neri

Neri begot Shealtiel

Shealtiel begot Zerubbabel

Zerubbabel begot Rhesa

Rhesa begot Joannas

Joannas begot Judah

Judah begot Joseph

Joseph begot Semei

Semei begot Mattathiah

Mattathiah begot Maath

Maath begot Naggai

Naggai begot Esli

Esli begot Nahum

Nahum begot Amos

Amos begot Mattathiah

Mattathiah begot Joseph

Joseph begot Janna

Janna begot Melchi

Melchi begot Levi

Levi begot Matthat

Matthat begot Heli

Heli begot Joseph the adoptive father of Jesus

Heli was Mary's father. Levirate law established the precedent to list the wife's husband in the genealogy. Thus Christ was also the direct seed of Mary, the ultimate Seed of the woman, and the lawful One to be the required kinsman redeemer. In fact, in the Hebrew, 'kinsman' is a synonym for 'redeemer.'

Thus we see a perfect prophecy perfectly fulfilled!

Preserving the royal lineage

The Bible provides detailed examples of the lengths that God would go to fulfill His word.

The following accounts represent other attempts by Satan to prevent the Seed of the woman from fulfilling God's promises.

During the period 853 – 841 BC Jehoram ruled in Judah. He was a very evil king who sought to preserve his kingship by killing all his brothers and other princes. That action nearly eliminated Judah's royal line. In addition Jehoram had married a daughter of Ahab named Athaliah.

"Nevertheless, because of the covenant the LORD had made with David, the LORD was not willing to destroy the house of David. He had promised to maintain a lamp for him and his descendants forever." 2 Chronicles 21:7 NIV

Recall King David was of the tribe of Judah, so David's offspring would be the offspring of Judah.

And while Jehoram was taking drastic steps to preserve his kingship, his days were about to be ended in pain according to the prophet Elijah.

And a letter came to him from Elijah the prophet saying:

"This is what the LORD, the God of your father David, says: 'You have not walked in the ways of your father Jehoshaphat or of Asa king of Judah. But you have walked in the ways of the kings of Israel, and you have led Judah and the people of Jerusalem to prostitute themselves, just as the house of Ahab did. You have also murdered your own brothers, members of your father's house, men who where better than you. So now the LORD is about to strike your people, your sons, your wives and everything that is yours, with a heavy blow. You yourself will be very ill with a lingering disease of the bowels (intestines), until the disease causes your bowels to come out.'" 2 Chronicles 21:12-15 NIV

Shortly thereafter, Elijah's prophecy relative to Jehoram took effect.

"In the course of time...his bowels came out because of the disease, and he died in great pain...He passed away, to no one's regret, and was buried in the City of David, but not in the tombs of the kings." 2 Chronicles 21:19-20 NIV

One small child

After Jehoram's death he was succeeded by his youngest son Ahaziah. Ahaziah was also evil and after reigning for less than a year was killed. His death caused his mother to take revenge.

"When Athaliah the mother of Ahaziah saw that her son was dead, she proceeded to destroy the whole royal family of the house of Judah. But Jehosheba, the daughter of King Jehoram, took Joash son of Ahaziah and stole him away from among the royal princes who were about to be murdered and put him and his nurse in a bedroom. Because Jehosheba, the daughter of King Jehoram and wife of the priest Jehoiada, was Ahaziah's sister, she hid the child from Athaliah so she could not kill him. He remained hidden with them at the temple of God for six years while Athaliah ruled the land." 2 Chronicles 22:10-12 NIV

The detail provided to protect the royal line of Judah is nearly incomprehensible, but so is God's plan and ways.

The royal line of Judah had been reduced to a single young child who was miraculously hidden in the very temple chambers for six years until evil Athaliah was killed.

"Joash was seven years when he became king, and he reigned in Jerusalem forty years....Joash did what was right in the eyes of the LORD..." 2 Chronicles 24:1-2 NIV

Rehoboam ruled in Judah   931-913 BC after the kingdom was divided
Abijah ruled in Judah   913-911 BC

Asa ruled in Judah	911-870 BC
Jehoshaphat ruled in Judah	873-848 BC three years co-regency
Jehoram ruled in Judah	853-841 BC five years co-regency
Ahaziah ruled in Judah	841 BC
Athaliah ruled in Judah	841-835 BC
Joash ruled in Judah	835-796 BC
Amaziah ruled in Judah	796-767 BC
Azaziah (Uzziah) ruled in Judah	790-739 BC twenty-three year's co-regency

Again, the historical writings such as 2 Chronicles do not contradict Christ's genealogy presented in Matthew; rather the historical books simply provide more detail.

For example Matthew states that Joram (Jehoram) begot Uzziah (Azariah). The book of 2 Chronicles provides the detailed lineage, i.e. Joram (Jehoram), Ahaziah, Athaliah (Queen), Joash, Amaziah, Azariah (Uzziah). Perfect harmony exists between the two accounts of Christ's lineage.

Another of Satan's attempts to eliminate the lineage of Judah, the tribe who would provide Israel's Redeemer, was foiled.

Without a doubt Satan was also trying to protect himself from the One who would ultimately destroy him. He remembered clearly the curse in the garden after he deceived the woman.

"Because you have done this...I will put enmity between you and the woman, and between your seed and her Seed; He shall bruise your head..." Genesis 3:14a, 15 NKJV

This wonderful story brings to mind some of the final words Jesus spoke to His disciples just before His ascension.

"...Everything must be fulfilled that is written about me in the Law of Moses, the Prophets and Psalms." Luke 24:44 NIV

God's plan for His chosen is right on schedule.

Chapter 9

Redemption for Israel –
God's Chosen Nation

After God gave instruction to Abram (Abraham) to leave his native land on the east of the Euphrates River to come to a new land that He would show him, He made the famous, immutable promise.

"I will make you into a great nation and I will bless you...and all peoples (families) on earth will be blessed through you." Genesis 12:2-3 NIV

That promise signified that Israel was/is/and always will be God's chosen and special nation above all other nations in any time in history - past, present, or future.

God reaffirmed that truth numerous times throughout both Old and New Testaments.

"...The LORD your God has chosen you out of all the peoples (families) on the face of the earth to be his people, his treasured possession." Deuteronomy 7:6 NIV

We have seen in great detail that God's promise to Abraham would be perpetuated and fulfilled through his descendants Isaac and Jacob.

Moses reminded Israel of their significance in the eyes of their God.

"Ask now about the former days, long before your time, from the day God created man on the earth; ask from one end of the heavens to the other. Has anything so great as this ever happened...Has any god ever tried to take for himself one nation out of another nation...?" Deuteronomy 4:32, 34 NIV

Moses tells Israel that since man was created, no nation or people have received the same attentive love and affection as they.

"You were shown these things so that you might know that the LORD is God; besides him there is no other. From heaven he made you hear his voice to discipline you..." Deuteronomy 4:35-36 NIV

God personally revealed Himself to Israel. He talked with them and instructed them in His righteousness and justice.

"Because he loved your forefathers and those their descendants after them..." Deuteronomy 4:37 NIV

And because God loved their fathers, i.e. Abraham, Isaac, and Jacob, His love and blessings would flow on down to and through their descendants.

"Acknowledge and take to heart this day that the LORD is God in heaven above and on the earth below. There is no other. Keep his decrees and commands..." Deuteronomy 4:39-40 NIV

God made it explicitly clear that there was no God other than Himself; therefore, the Israelites were expected to keep His commandments.

Israel continues to disobey

Throughout their history, Israel disobeyed God's commandments and was continually chastised; however, the thought of forsaking them never entered the mind of God.

In fact, God continually reassured Israel that they were His chosen, regardless of their disobedience and their resulting unpleasant circumstances.

Seven hundred years after Moses death, God reassured Israel of their favored status.

"But you, Israel, are My servant, Jacob whom I have chosen, the descendants of Abraham My friend. You whom I have taken from the ends of the earth...and said to you, 'You are My servant, I have chosen you and have not cast

you away: Fear not, for I am with you...' For I, the LORD your God, will hold your right hand, saying to you, 'fear not, I will help you.'" Isaiah 41:8-10a, 13-14 NKJV

God reminded Israel that regardless of their circumstances and plight, He would never leave them or forget the promises He made to Abraham, Isaac, and Jacob (Israel). God reaffirmed the fact that Israel was His chosen.

God has/is and will unquestionably in the future fulfill His promises to Abraham and perfect His plan for His chosen nation.

The prophet Amos, a contemporary of Isaiah, confirmed Israel's favored status; however, he also reminded them that God would by His nature deal with their disobedience.

"Hear this word the LORD has spoken against you, O people of Israel – against the whole family I brought up out of Egypt: 'You only have I chosen of all the families of the earth; therefore I will punish you for all your sins.'" Amos 3:1-2 NIV

Even though Israel is God's chosen, God must by His Holy nature, speak out against Israel and punish them for their sin, as confirmed by the word 'therefore.' This passage ends with another profound 'I will;' i.e. "I will punish you for all your iniquities."

Redemption for God's chosen nation

When a person or nation is literally enslaved or in bondage, that person or nation can at God's option be redeemed from such slavery or bondage. In addition when a person or nation is enslaved to the bondage of sin, that person or nation can, again at God's option, be redeemed from that depraved position.

Such was the case of God's chosen nation. Their favored status in the eyes of their God did not eliminate their need for redemption; in fact only God's chosen will partake of redemption.

It is an extremely significant fact that redemption can only be done by God; i.e. man is totally impotent to redeem himself or others.

"Hear this, all peoples; give ear, all inhabitants of the world, both low and high, rich and poor together...none of them can by any means redeem his brother, nor give to God a ransom for him – for the redemption of their souls is costly...but God will redeem my soul from the power of the grave, for He shall receive me." Psalm 49:1-2, 7-8, 15 NKJV

This passage does not refer to the redemption of property or the redemption of a relative from slavery. Rather it refers exclusively to the redemption of one's soul. Only God can redeem one's soul from the power of the grave.

And just as the Bible emphasizes repeatedly the fact that Israel is God's chosen nation, Israel is also chastised repeatedly due to continuing sin. The Bible also speaks repeatedly of Israel's redemption.

It will be shown that Israel was redeemed from their bondage in Egypt; redeemed from their subsequent seventy years of exile in Babylon; and redeemed from their repeated sins of disobedience.

"But now, this is what the LORD says – he who created you, O Jacob, he who formed you, O Israel: 'Fear not, for I have redeemed you; I have summoned you by name, you are mine...For I am the LORD, your God, the Holy One of Israel, your Savior; I give Egypt for your ransom...I even I, am the LORD, and apart from me there is no savior.'" Isaiah 43:1, 3, 11 NIV

God reminded Israel that they were His creation and He was the One who redeemed them from their Egyptian bondage. He reaffirmed Israel's favored status and the fact that there was no one else who could save them.

"But now listen, O Jacob, my servant, Israel, whom I have chosen...This is what the LORD says – Israel's King and Redeemer... 'I am the first and I am the last; apart from me there is no God.'" Isaiah 44:1, 6 NIV

God reaffirms Israel as His chosen. He refers to Himself as the King of Israel along with being their Redeemer. He then reaffirms His omnipotence.

"Listen to me, O Jacob, Israel, whom I have called...My own hand laid the foundations of the earth...This is what the LORD says – your Redeemer, the Holy One of Israel... Leave Babylon...Announce this with shouts of joy and proclaim it. Send it out to the ends of the earth; say, 'The LORD has redeemed his servant Jacob.'" Isaiah 48:12-13, 17, 20 NIV

God refers to Israel as His called and announces their redemption from Babylonian captivity. He instructs Israel to announce to the whole earth that it was their God who redeemed them. Israel's redemption from historical Babylon has end time implications.

God also refers to Himself as being a husband to Israel, in addition to His being their Redeemer.

"For your Maker is your husband – the Holy One of Israel is your Redeemer; he is called the God of all the earth. The LORD will call you back as if you were a wife deserted and distressed (forsaken and grieved) in spirit... 'For a brief moment I abandoned (have forsaken) you, but with deep compassion I will bring you back. In a surge of anger I hid my face from you for a moment, but with everlasting kindness I will have compassion on you,' says the LORD your Redeemer." Isaiah 54:5-8 NIV

The Hebrew word translated 'forsaken' in the above means 'to relinquish,' 'set free,' or 'to release someone to do as they wish.'

God rescues a forsaken nation as a husband rescues a grieving and forsaken wife. The significance of this passage is that God is required by His nature to forsake sin and show His wrath; but for His chosen His wrath is only for a moment, while His kindness and mercy will last forever.

God reiterated to Isaiah that Israel would also possess the land forever.

"Your sun will never set again, and your moon will wane no more; the LORD will be your everlasting light, and your days of sorrow will end. Then will all your people be righteous and they will possess the land forever." Isaiah 60:20-21a NIV

Therefore, Israel as a nation and as a people will remain forever.

"'As the new heavens and the new earth that I make will endure before me,' says the LORD, 'so will your name and descendants endure (remain).'" Isaiah 66:22 NIV

The holy city of Jerusalem was/is also in need of redemption, as is the nation of which she is the capital.

"The LORD has made proclamation to the ends of the earth: 'Say to the Daughter of Zion, "See, your Savior comes! See, his reward is with him, and his recompense accompanies him."' They will be called the Holy People, the Redeemed of the LORD, and you will be called Sought

After, the City No longer Deserted (forsaken)." Isaiah 62:11-12 NIV

In the future, Jerusalem will be redeemed permanently from her harlotry.

After centuries of disobedience, wandering, chastisement, and unrest Israel would come to their senses.

"They remembered that God was their Rock, that God Most High was their Redeemer." Psalm 78:35 NIV

God in the flesh would redeem Israel

In the days of King Ahaz, king of Judah, there was much unrest, due to persistent pressure from Rezin king of Syria and Pekah king of Israel (Northern tribes), who sought to make war against Judah by marching on Jerusalem. God told Isaiah to assure Ahaz that the enemy would not prevail. Ahaz, however, was still skeptical; so God offered to provide a sign to Ahaz to prove His sovereignty.

"Therefore the LORD himself will give you a sign: The virgin will be with child and will give birth to a son, and will call him Immanuel." Isaiah 7:14 NIV

Isaiah then provides further details about the Son to be born of a virgin.

"For unto us a child is born, to us a son is given, and the government will be on his shoulders. And he will be

called...Mighty God, Everlasting Father, Prince of Peace."
Isaiah 9:6 NIV

Isaiah revealed that the Son would be deity, i.e. God Himself in the flesh. Inasmuch as the Son would be given, there must be a specific purpose for His appearance as a man on the earth. That purpose is partially revealed, inasmuch as the government would rest on His shoulder.

"Of the increase of his government and peace there will be no end. He will reign on David's throne and over his kingdom, establishing and upholding it with justice and righteousness...The zeal of the LORD Almighty will accomplish this." Isaiah 9:7 NIV

God will administer justice on the earth through the coming King, who would be of the family of David who was of the family of Abraham, Isaac, and Jacob. Of great interest is that God has a great zeal to fulfill His plan.

Isaiah continues to provide more details about the God/ Man of the family of David.

"A shoot will come up from the stump of Jesse; from his roots a Branch will bear fruit. The Spirit of the LORD will rest on him – the Spirit of wisdom and of understanding..." Isaiah 11:1-2 NIV

As stated in chapter 8, Jesse was the father of David who was the great grandson of Boaz who redeemed Naomi's husband's family name and lost possession. Jesus Christ is the ultimate Root of Jesse through Jesse's son David.

"I, Jesus, have sent my angel to give you this testimony for the churches. I am the Root and the Offspring of David..." Revelation 22:16 NIV

Jesus Christ, as deity, was the ultimate Root of David; and inasmuch as He was/is the Man, He is also of the physical seed, or offspring, of David.

Israel's Redeemer is given for all nations

Note that Isaiah reveals that the Gentiles shall also seek Him in addition to Israel.

"Here is my servant, whom I uphold, my chosen one in whom I delight; I will put my Spirit on him and he will bring justice to the nations (Gentiles) ...I, the LORD, have called you in righteousness; I will take hold of your hand. I will keep you and will make you to be a covenant for the people and a light for the Gentiles." Isaiah 42:1, 6 NIV

Again, God reveals that His Son will not only save Israel, but the Gentiles as well. God will 'give' Him for all peoples, Jew and Gentile.

"...he says: 'It is too small a thing for you to be my servant to restore the tribes of Jacob and bring back those of Israel I have kept. I will also make you a light for the

Gentiles, that you may bring my salvation to the ends of the earth.'" Isaiah 49:6 NIV

This verse contains numerous profound truths. The remnant of Israel comes first, but then God's Servant the Messiah would be given as a light (enlightenment) to all peoples so that God's salvation would reach to all the ends of the earth. These words fulfill God's promise to Abraham that he would be a blessing to all the families of the earth.

And then in the New Testament when the Prophet Simeon held Jesus in his arms, he uttered a profound prophecy.

"For my eyes have seen your salvation, which you have prepared in the sight of all people, a light for revelation to the Gentiles and for glory to your people Israel." Luke 2:30-32 NIV

Israel's Redeemer is born

Recall when the son of Zacharias, i.e. John the Baptist, was circumcised, Zacharias proclaimed John's role. His Spirit-induced prophecy acknowledged that John would be the prophet of the Highest. Zacharias' prophecy began by stating the Redeemer of Israel, for whom John would be the forerunner, was about to appear.

"Blessed is the Lord God of Israel, for He has visited and redeemed His people, and has raised up a horn of salvation for us in the house of His servant David, as He

spoke by the mouth of His holy prophets, who have been since the world began..." Luke 1:68-70 NKJV

Even after Jesus' death and resurrection, many Jews didn't recognize Him as their Redeemer. Recall on the Emmaus Road Cleopas was confessing to Jesus, who at that point wasn't recognized by Cleopas, that he had hoped that the crucified Christ was Israel's redeemer.

"...but we had hoped that he was the one who was going to redeem Israel. And what is more, it is the third day since all this took place. In addition, some of our women amazed us. They went to the tomb early this morning but didn't find his body." Luke 24:21-23a NIV

Jesus, still not recognized by Cleopas, explained the recent events.

"He said to them, 'How foolish you are, and how slow of heart to believe all that the prophets have spoken! Did not the Christ have to suffer these things and then enter his glory?' And beginning with Moses and all the Prophets, he explained to them what was said in all the Scriptures concerning himself." Luke 24:25-27 NIV

Shortly thereafter Jesus addressed the eleven and reiterated that all that was said of Him in the entirety of the Old Testament must be fulfilled.

"...Everything must be fulfilled that is written about me in the Law of Moses, the Prophets and the Psalms...This

is what is written: The Christ will suffer and rise from the dead on the third day, and repentance and forgiveness (remission) of sins will be preached in his name to all nations, beginning at Jerusalem." Luke 24:44, 46-47 NIV

The Greek for 'remission' in the above is *aphesis* meaning 'to release one's sins from the sinner.' Synonyms include 'redemption,' 'freedom,' 'deliverance,' 'propitiation,' and 'justification.'

Recall Jesus' words to His disciples on a previous occasion:

"...just as the Son of Man did not come to be served, but to serve, and to give his life as a ransom for many." Matthew 20:28 NIV

The Greek for 'ransom' in the above is *antilutron* meaning 'the price of redemption.' It is also synonymous with 'freedom.'

Jesus made it very clear that He was the object of the Old Testament and everything said of Him would be fulfilled to the letter.

Israel's redeemed (chosen) is a remnant

The concept of 'remnant' is closely related to the term 'few' which is defined in both Hebrew and Greek as 'remainder' or 'what is left over,' or 'remaining from the whole.'

'Remnant' from the Hebrew *yathar* does in fact mean the 'smaller part of the whole.' Synonyms include 'remainder' and 'residue.'

The term 'remnant' is found numerous times in the Scriptures to describe the redeemed, or chosen, of Israel.

"In that day the remnant of Israel, the survivors of the house of Jacob, will no longer rely on him who struck them down but will truly rely on the LORD, the Holy One of Israel. A remnant will return, a remnant of Jacob will return to the Mighty God. Though your people, O Israel, be like the sand by the sea, only a remnant will return." Isaiah 10:20-22 NIV

The phrase 'in that day' refers to the millennial kingdom when Israel will cease depending on other nations for their safety and general well being but will rather depend wholly on God. Only a small portion, or remnant, of total Israel will return to God.

Israel realized that, if not for the grace of God, there would not be even a remnant.

"Unless the LORD of hosts had left to us a very small remnant, we would have become like Sodom..." Isaiah 1:9 NKJV

Note the remnant in this passage is described as 'very small.'

Approximately 200 years after Isaiah, God spoke to Ezekiel about Israel's harlotry, but reminded him that a small remnant would be saved to proclaim His name among the nations.

"Yet I will leave a remnant, so that you may have some who escape the sword among the nations, when you are scattered through the countries. Then those of you who escape will remember Me among the nations where they are carried captive, because I was crushed by their adulterous heart which has departed from Me, and by their eyes which play the harlot after their idols..." Ezekiel 6:8-9 NKJV

Thus, a remnant of the seed of Israel will exist as a nation forever, while the majority will be destroyed. The Bible also sheds light on the size of the chosen remnant of Israel who will enjoy millennial and eternal blessings.

"On that day a fountain will be opened to the house of David... 'In the whole land,' declares the LORD, 'two-thirds will be struck down and perish; yet one-third will be left in it...They will call on my name and I will answer them;' I will say, 'They are my people...'" Zechariah 13:1, 8-9 NIV

Zechariah confirms Isaiah's prophecy that a remnant of Israel will be delivered into the millennial kingdom. Zechariah, however, quantifies the remnant as being one-third of those surviving at the time of Christ's return.

As would be expected, the New Testament confirms Old Testament teachings. Paul in fact quotes a portion of Isaiah's prophecy about the remnant of Israel.

"Isaiah cries out concerning Israel: 'Though the number of the Israelites be like the sand by the sea, only the remnant will be saved.'" Romans 9:27 NIV

Paul loved the Jews, inasmuch as he was one by birth, being in the lineage of Abraham through Isaac and Jacob and Benjamin. He wrote extensively about Israel's future in his epistle to the Christians in Rome.

"I ask then: 'Did God reject his people? By no means! ...God did not reject his people, whom he foreknew.'" Romans 11:1-2 NIV

Paul goes on to explain that when Elijah thought he was the only one remaining who was faithful to God, God responded by revealing that there were 7,000 who remained faithful to Him. Paul continued by stating that God has always preserved a remnant of Israel.

"So too, at the present time there is a remnant chosen by grace." Roman 11:5 NIV

The redemption of the remnant of Israel is one of the keystone teachings of the Bible. It is a sad commentary that many today in the 'church' are beginning to turn their backs on Israel by way of replacement theology. Such thinking that the church has taken Israel's place as the recipient of God's immutable promises never entered the mind of God.

Many present day millennials, i.e. those born between 1982 and 2004, are beginning to think that Israel is more of a problem in the Middle East than a blessing.

Such is blatant heresy.

Consider further that in America today, approximately 75% of the population claim they are Christians. Many would, therefore, conclude that this same percentage of Americans would be delivered from destruction.

However, is there any reason to believe that a larger percentage of Americans would be saved than one-third of Israelites?

Recall what God said to Israel.

"For you are a people holy to the LORD your God. The LORD your God has chosen you out of all the peoples on the face of the earth to be his people, his treasured possession." Deuteronomy 7:6 NIV

No other nation has been awarded such status.

Chapter 10

Redemption for the Church

The Bible reveals that the redemptive price that Christ paid for Israel is sufficient to redeem God's chosen from all nations, tribes, tongues, etc.

The meaning of 'redemption' in the Greek is very similar to its meaning in Hebrew, i.e. 'to release on receipt of ransom,' 'to deliver,' 'to rescue completely,' and 'to set free.'

"Christ redeemed us from the curse of the law by becoming a curse for us...that the blessing given to Abraham might come to the Gentiles through Christ Jesus, so that by faith we might receive the promise of the Spirit." Galatians 3:13-14 NIV

The nation of Israel and the church are two very different and distinct entities. However, both are the objects of God's choosing, and each has a prominent role in His eternal, immutable plan. And while both are distinctly different, both require redemption because both have violated God's laws and both are/were enslaved to sin.

Paul succinctly addressed these issues in his letter to the church in Galatia.

"So also, when we were children, we were in slavery under the basic principles of the world. But when the time had fully come, God sent his Son, born of a woman, born under law, to redeem those under law, that we might receive the full rights of sons." Galatians 4:3-5 NIV

Paul explains that members of the church were also previously under the law, i.e. God's standard of righteousness and justice is universal to all mankind, applicable to national Israel as well to all non-Israelites. After individuals place their faith in Christ, they are free from the condemnation of the law because Christ fulfilled the law and paid the sinner's debt.

"In Him you also trusted, after you heard the word of truth, the gospel of your salvation, in whom also, having believed, you were sealed with the Holy Spirit of promise, who is the guarantee of our inheritance until the redemption of the purchased possession..." Ephesians 1:13-14 NKJV

Paul explains that after one hears the word and believes, they are sealed with the Holy Spirit. To be 'sealed' means to 'attest,' i.e. 'confirm authenticity.' A synonymous phrase is 'to render secure.' Such a seal is in essence the down payment of one's inheritance.

The Christian is the purchased possession. The redemptive process will be completed when they receive their glorified body. After one believes, the redemptive process has begun, and nothing can thwart God's plan.

Paul later instructs Christians to live their lives in obedience on the road to their final destiny.

"And do not grieve the Holy Spirit of God, with who you were sealed for the day of redemption." Ephesians 4:30 NIV

The redemptive price paid for the church is the same price paid to ransom Israel

Luke affirms the redemptive price paid for the New Testament church.

"...Be shepherds of the church of God, which he bought (purchased) with his own blood." Acts 20:28b NIV

The Greek for 'purchased' means 'to gain for oneself;' a people acquired or purchased in a peculiar or unique manner. Yes indeed, the unique manner was to acquire for Himself His chosen people by ransoming them from sin with the payment of the blood of His only Son.

The great truth that Christ paid the redemptive price for mankind with His own blood pervades the entire New Testament.

"Since we have now been justified by his blood, how much more shall we be saved from God's wrath through him!" Romans 5:9 NIV

The meaning of 'justified' is 'to be declared righteous' by faith in Christ and not by the works of the law.

"Not only is this so, but we also rejoice in God through our Lord Jesus Christ, through whom we have now received reconciliation." Romans 5:11 NIV

Man is adjudicated not guilty and portrayed as reconciled to God through the death of Christ. The Greek 'reconciled' means the restoration of a relationship which had been damaged because of man's sin.

"In him we have redemption through his blood, the forgiveness of sins, in accordance with the riches of God's grace..." Ephesians 1:7 NIV

Once again, Paul declares that the blood of Christ was the redemptive price paid for man's sins, and His offering was a gift.

"In him we were also chosen, having been predestined according to the plan of him who works out everything in conformity with the purpose of his will..." Ephesians 1:11 NIV

Inasmuch as the redemptive price has been paid and accepted, those of faith have been given an inheritance which was all part of God's master plan for those created in His own image before the foundation of the world.

"He has delivered us from the power of darkness and conveyed us into the kingdom of the Son of His love, in whom we have redemption through His blood, the forgiveness of sins." Colossians 1:13-14 NKJV

Recall 'delivered' and 'redemption' are synonyms. Once again Paul confirms the redemptive price paid was the blood offered by Christ, i.e. the Son of God's love.

"For God was pleased to have all his fullness dwell in him, and through him to reconcile to himself all things on earth or things in heaven, by making peace through his blood, shed on the cross." Colossians 1:19-20 NIV

It pleased God to offer the blood of Christ to reconcile 'all things' to Himself. This was an integral part of God's plan for man, which He devised before man was ever created.

The blood of Jesus' cross confirms the humanity of Christ, while the wording 'in Him all the fullness should dwell' confirms the deity of Christ. What a magnificent plan for God's chosen!

The writer of Hebrews explains the fulfillment of the Old Testament law regarding atonement by blood. The old covenant had to be fulfilled by the new covenant.

Both center on the offering of blood which represents the payment for sin. Recall there is no forgiveness without shedding of blood. All sin must be reckoned with and paid for.

"...you were bought at a price." 1 Corinthians 6:20a NIV

"When Christ came as high priest...He did not enter by means of the blood of goats and calves; but he entered the Most Holy Place once for all by his own blood, having obtained eternal redemption." Hebrews 9:11-12 NIV

The Old Testament consistently provided types that enable God's chosen to understand and grasp the magnificence of the New Testament and the new covenant. Note the power in the above passage where the writer explains that God's chosen has obtained 'eternal redemption' by the blood of Christ.

The blood of animals was just a type preparing for the perfect sacrifice. The type was originally illustrated when God clothed Adam and Eve with skins of animals.

Recall the stern warning for those who take lightly God's plan and the offering of His Son.

"How much more severely do you think a man deserves to be punished who has trampled the Son of God under foot, who has treated as an unholy thing the blood of the covenant that sanctified him, and who has insulted the Spirit of grace?" Hebrews 10:29 NIV

Paul also confessed that his teaching centered on Christ and His cross.

It is noteworthy to keep in mind that the Bible and its prophecies will be fulfilled in terms of Jewish law.

Redemption – present and future

We've already seen that God's chosen are redeemed from the bondage and curse of the law, but redemption involves even more.

"Grace and peace to you from God our Father and the Lord Jesus Christ, who gave himself for our sins to rescue us from the present age, according to the will of our God and Father..." Galatians 1:3-4 NIV

It was God's will that His chosen would be protected during this present evil age. The enemy has no power over God's people.

Peter reminded Christ's followers that their redemption was not based on temporal things.

"For you know that it was not with perishable things such as silver or gold that you were redeemed...but with the precious blood of Christ, a lamb without blemish or defect. He was chosen before the creation (foundation) of the world, but was revealed in these last times for your sake." 1 Peter 1:18-20 NIV

Paul then explained that the Christian also eagerly waits for the redemption of his corruptible body to an incorruptible glorified body.

"Not only so, but we ourselves, who have the firstfruits of the Spirit, groan inwardly as we wait eagerly for our adoption as sons, the redemption of our bodies." Romans 8:23 NIV

Therefore, the redemption price has been paid; the Christian is just waiting for the final step of glorification of the body and renewal of the earth.

Chapter 11

The Nations in God's Plan

God's numerous "I will" proclamations recorded in the early chapters of the Bible include many directed to the 'nations.' Recall the predominant Hebrew word for 'nations' in the Old Testament is *goy* which refers primarily to gentiles or heathen, i.e. non Jews.

Nations are first mentioned relative to the sons of Noah in the early chapters of Genesis. For example, after the descendants of the three sons of Noah are listed, along with their dwelling places, the following is stated:

"These were the families of the sons of Noah, according to their generations, in their nations; and from these the nations were divided on the earth after the flood." Genesis 10:32 NKJV

Recall that God told Abram that He would make him a great nation and in so doing all the families of the earth would be blessed. As previously noted, the word 'family' is more narrowly defined as a kindred or tribe within a nation.

Inasmuch as 'nations' are one of the key components of God's master plan, details of their participation in God's plan can be found throughout the Scriptures from Genesis to Revelation. A remnant from all nations will exist in perpetuity.

Nations – geographic significance

When the word 'nations' is found in the Old Testament, the context must be examined. The Hebrew basis for the word 'nations' can also be used interchangeably with the words 'country' and 'land.' A great example is found in Ezekiel.

"Thus says the Lord God: 'Surely I will take the children of Israel from among the nations, wherever they have gone, and will gather them from every side and bring them into their own land; and I will make them one nation in the land...Then they shall dwell in the land that I have given to Jacob My servant, where your fathers dwelt; and they shall dwell there, they, their children, and their children's children, forever; and My servant David shall be their prince forever.'" Ezekiel 37:21-22, 25 NKJV

Thus the people of God's chosen nation will be gathered from all corners of the earth and dwell in the physical land promised to their fathers forever.

Moses also acknowledged that God determined national boundaries.

"When the Most High divided their inheritance to the nations...He set the boundaries of the peoples according to the number of the children of Israel." Deuteronomy 32:8 NKJV

And in the New Testament, Paul confirmed God's providence in establishing boundaries for the nations.

"And He has made...every nation of men to dwell on all the face of the earth, and has determined...the boundaries of their dwellings..." Acts 17:26 NKJV

Israel's Redeemer/Messiah/King will in God's timing rule all nations

"...The LORD has said to Me, You are My Son...Ask of Me, and I will give You the nations (heathen) for Your inheritance...You shall break them with a rod of iron..." Psalm 2:7-9 NKJV

This proclamation will be exactly fulfilled upon the return of Christ to earth to end the tribulation.

Continuing in Psalms it is written that the nations are naïve; their plans amount to nothing. Their best option is to place their trust totally in God.

"The LORD brings the counsel of the nations to nothing; He makes the plans of the peoples of no effect. The counsel of the LORD stands forever, the plans of His heart to all generations. Blessed is the nation whose God is the LORD,

the people He has chosen as His own inheritance." Psalm 33:10-12 NKJV

Much is found in the books of the prophets about the nations from Isaiah to Malachi.

"Now it shall come to pass in the latter days that the mountain of the LORD's house shall be established on the top of the mountains...and all nations shall flow to it." Isaiah 2:2 NKJV

Throughout history all nations were/are subject to the sovereign rule of God, and they would respond to whatever He calls them to do. God uses nations to bless and/or to chastise Israel for His purpose. There is really no such thing as a sovereign nation.

"He will lift up a banner to the nations from afar; and will whistle to them from the end of the earth; surely they shall come with speed, swiftly." Isaiah 5:26 NKJV

Even the nations that hate Israel in this present age will at the appointed time in the future, seek the King and Ruler of Israel. Those that will not serve Israel's future King will perish.

"The Gentiles shall come to your light, and kings to the brightness of your rising...the wealth of the Gentiles shall come to you. The multitude of camels shall cover your land, the dromedaries of Midian and Ephah; all those from Sheba shall come...all the flocks of Kedar shall be gathered

together to you, the rams of Nebaioth shall minister to you...for the nation and kingdom which will not serve you shall perish and those nations shall be utterly ruined." Isaiah 60:3, 6-7, 12 NKJV

The nations listed above are primarily from the Arabian Peninsula and offspring of Ishmael, and/or sons of Keturah. The tiny nation of Israel that appears to be fighting for her survival in today's hostile world will be the central point of the entire earth at the appointed time in the future.

The nations that are presently enemies of Israel will bow to King Jesus or face utter ruin.

The prophet Jeremiah also spoke of the nations. He reiterated the truth that the nations with all their wisdom are as nothing compared with God.

"Inasmuch as there is none like You...Who would not fear You, O King of the nations? For this is Your rightful due. For among all the wise men of the nations, and in all their kingdoms, there is none like You. But they are altogether dull-hearted and foolish..." Jeremiah 10:6-8 NKJV

Following the tribulation period, during the millennial kingdom, all nations will journey to Jerusalem to pay homage to Israel's King and Messiah. That is further proof that the nations will endure forever.

The redeemed of all nations will honor the King of Israel

Zechariah, a post-exilic prophet, also had much to say about the nations:

"Many nations shall be joined to the LORD in that day, and they shall become My people. And I will dwell in your midst. Then you will know that the LORD of hosts has sent Me to you. And the LORD will take possession of Judah as His inheritance in the Holy Land, and will again choose Jerusalem." Zechariah 2:11-12 NKJV

In this passage God is addressing Jerusalem, and even though many nations will become God's people in the future, those nations will in no way replace Israel as God's most treasured nation. The passage also confirms the Biblical truth that God will dwell in Jerusalem forever.

Zechariah addresses that very issue in the following:

"Yes, many peoples and strong nations shall come to seek the LORD of hosts in Jerusalem and to pray before the LORD. Thus says the LORD of hosts, 'In those days ten men from every language of the nations shall grasp the sleeve of a Jewish man,' saying, 'Let us go with you, for we have heard that God is with you.'" Zechariah 8:22-23 NKJV

And finally, the last prophet to write in the Old Testament, i.e. Malachi, wrote of the nations worshipping the one and true God.

"For from the rising of the sun, even to its going down, My name shall be great among the Gentiles; in every place incense shall be offered to My name, and a pure offering; for My name shall be great among the nations." Malachi 1:11 NKJV

Judgment of the nations

The prophet Joel wrote of God judging all nations in His pre-planned time table.

"For behold, in those days and at that time, when I bring back the captives of Judah and Jerusalem, I will also gather all nations, and bring them down to the Valley of Jehoshaphat; and I will enter into judgment with them there on account of My people, My heritage Israel, whom they have scattered among the nations; they have also divided up My land." Joel 3:1-2 NKJV

After the tribulation period God will gather the dispersed of Judah and Jerusalem and return them to their homeland. At that time He will also gather all nations into Israel and judge them for their treatment of the Jews.

The nations should remember that Israel was, is, and always will be the apple of God's eye.

Notice also that God mentions one of the sins of the nations, i.e. they have divided the land of Israel. Consider presently that the single option offered for peace in the

Middle East is for Israel to give up part of their land to a sovereign Palestinian state in their midst.

Consider the present division of Israel where the Palestinians occupy and partially control Gaza and the West Bank.

In late 2012 the UN General Assembly passed resolution 67/19 upgrading Palestine to 'non-member observer state status.' The action was considered 'de facto recognition of the sovereign state of Palestine.' The terrorist group Hamas is intimately involved in the governance of what is called the Palestinian territory of Gaza.

According to the Bible, any proposal to divide the land promised to Abraham and his seed is absurd. The truth is that the Palestinians do not want to share the land with the Jews; they want to totally destroy God's chosen people. Of course, according to the word of God, that will never happen.

The argument is even more interesting considering that the Ottomans previously controlled the West Bank for four centuries ending in 1917.

It is all part of the ongoing battle between Abraham's sons Isaac and Ishmael. The battle of the brothers rages on.

All nations will hear the gospel message

The prophet Isaiah tells that God will reveal Himself to all nations so that all might witness His salvation.

"The LORD has made bare His holy arm in the eyes of all the nations, and all the ends of the earth shall see the salvation of our God." Isaiah 52:10 NKJV

Moving along to the New Testament, the gospel writers confirm that the gospel of Jesus Christ would be proclaimed to all nations.

"And this gospel of the kingdom will be preached in all the world as a witness to all the nations, and then the end will come." Matthew 24:14 NKJV

Note that while the prophets spoke of the nations coming to Christ after the tribulation period, the gospel writers wrote of the preaching during the church age prior to the tribulation.

Later it will be shown that the final gospel message will also be spread throughout the world during the tribulation period.

Luke's message was similar to Matthew's.

"Then He (Christ) said to them, 'Thus it is written, and thus it was necessary for the Christ to suffer and to rise from the dead the third day, and that repentance and

remission of sins should be preached in His name to all nations, beginning at Jerusalem...'" Luke 24:46-47 NKJV

The whole world would hear the simple gospel truth that it was necessary for Christ to suffer and pay man's sin debt because no man could satisfy God's required righteousness. Christ arose as proof that God was satisfied with His Son's vicarious sacrifice.

The initial message of John the Baptist was repentance and remission of sins. That message would be spread abroad to all nations. Note also that the preaching of the message would begin in Jerusalem.

And sure enough, the church began at Jerusalem.

"And there were dwelling in Jerusalem Jews, devout men, from every nation under heaven..." Acts 2:5 NKJV

Representatives from every nation were gathered together and they were all amazed as they heard the gospel message in their native tongue.

"Then they were all amazed and marveled, saying to one another, 'Look, are not all these who speak Galileans? And how is it that we hear, each in our own language in which we were born?'" Acts 2:7-8 NKJV

During the early days of the church, Peter confirmed that those from any and all nations could participate in the Kingdom of God.

"Then Peter opened his mouth and said: 'In truth I perceive that God shows no partiality. But in every nation whoever fears Him and works righteousness is accepted by Him.'" Acts 10:34-35 NKJV

Nations during the great tribulation

Beginning in the 4th chapter of Revelation, John is taken to heaven in the Spirit and is able to view what is to take place in the future, i.e. after the present age of the church.

"After these things I looked, and behold, a door standing open in heaven. And the first voice which I heard was like a trumpet speaking with me, saying, 'Come up here, and I will show you things which must take place after this.' Immediately I was in the Spirit; and behold, a throne set in heaven, and One sat on the throne." Revelation 4:1-2 NKJV

John 'saw' many things including the results of the worldwide evangelism efforts spoken by Jesus. Recall Jesus, after His resurrection but before His ascension, told His disciples that the gospel would be preached to all nations.

John described his vision of the multitude of those martyred during the tribulation period.

"After these things I looked, and behold, a great multitude which no one could number, of all nations, tribes, peoples, and tongues, standing before the throne and before the Lamb... 'These are the ones who come out of the great

tribulation, and washed their robes and made them white in the blood of the Lamb.'" Revelation 7:9, 14 NKJV

The Bible teaches repeatedly that there is no partiality with God. The above certainly confirms that great truth. John takes great effort to explain that redemption by the blood of Christ has been made available to every segment of mankind, i.e. all nations, tribes, peoples, and tongues.

All nations will witness God's working in Jerusalem during the tribulation period

Shortly thereafter John was told of the two witnesses who were called to prophesy for 3 ½ years and would then be killed. Their dead bodies would lie in the streets for 3 ½ days and the entire earth would be able to view them.

"Then those from the peoples, tribes, tongues, and nations will see their dead bodies three-and-a-half days, and not allow their dead bodies to be put into graves." Revelation 11:9 NKJV

Again, every segment of mankind will view this event in real time and witness God's omnipotence unfolding before their eyes.

Such technology is already in operation as evidenced by the whole world viewing the beheading of innocents in the Middle East beginning in the summer of 2014.

God grants temporary power to the enemy to accomplish His eternal plan for all nations

Then John tells of the power and authority over the entire earth that would be given to the anti-Christ for a short time to accomplish God's purpose from the foundation of the world.

"It was granted to him to make war with the saints and to overcome them. And authority was given him over every tribe, tongue, and nation. All who dwell on the earth will worship him, whose names have not been written in the Book of Life of the Lamb slain from the foundation of the world." Revelation 13:7-8 NKJV

God's plan includes making Himself known to everyone on the earth; regardless in which generation they live. And so it will be during the most devastating days on earth, i.e. the latter half of the great tribulation period. Recall Jesus' words to describe the great tribulation.

"For then there will be great tribulation, such as has not been since the beginning of the world until this time, no, nor ever shall be." Matthew 24:21 NKJV

A final warning is given to all peoples before the final days of the great tribulation.

"Then I saw another angel flying in the midst of heaven, having the everlasting gospel to preach to those who dwell on the earth – to every nation, tribe, tongue, and

people – saying with a loud voice, 'Fear God and give glory to Him, for the hour of His judgment has come; and worship Him who made heaven and earth...'" Revelation 14:6-7 NKJV

And then seven angels who had the seven last plagues, called the seven bowls, were told to deliver the final judgments on the earth.

"Then I heard a loud voice from the temple saying to the seven angels, 'Go and pour out the bowls of the wrath of God on the earth.'" Revelation 16:1 NKJV

A major point to be made is that every segment of mankind from every generation will have been forewarned of God's righteousness and required wrath for those who choose not to fear the One who created all things, including them.

The enemy, however, would make one last unsuccessful attempt to deceive the nations at the end of the millennial kingdom.

"Now when the thousand years have expired, Satan will be released from his prison and will go out to deceive the nations which are in the four corners of the earth..." Revelation 20:7 NKJV

Many will in fact be deceived, but will be quickly destroyed along with the great deceiver.

"...to gather them together to battle, whose number is as the sand of the sea. They went up on the breadth of the earth and surrounded the camp of the saints and the beloved city, and fire came down from God out of heaven and devoured them." Revelation 20:8b-9 NKJV

In the final chapters of Revelation it is revealed that there are peoples of all segments of mankind enjoying the fulfillment of God's plan for man. As John is describing New Jerusalem which had descended from heaven, he notes the presence of those saved, but not of the church age.

"The city had no need of the sun or of the moon to shine in it, for the glory of God illuminated it. The Lamb is its light. And the nations shall walk in its light, and the kings of the earth bring their glory and honor into it." Revelation 21:23-24 NKJV

The redeemed of all nations will experience God's goodness

And the saved of all nations will partake of God's goodness and provision throughout all eternity. God will, once again, be dwelling with His highest creation, i.e. redeemed man.

The word 'saved' above is from the Greek *sozo* meaning 'deliver, make whole, and to preserve safely.' In the present context it specifically means 'salvation' and 'eternal life' by the vicarious death of Christ.

Recall the words of the new song which the four living creatures and the twenty-four elders sang after it was revealed that the Root of David, the Lion of the tribe of Judah, was worthy to loose the seven sealed scroll and complete the redemption of all people and all creation.

"You are worthy to take the scroll, and to open its seals; for You were slain, and have redeemed us to God by Your blood out of every tribe and tongue and people and nation, and have made us kings and priests to our God; and we shall reign on the earth." Revelation 5:9-10 NKJV

Without question, the promise made to Abraham in the early chapters of Genesis, that all families of all nations of the earth would be blessed through him, would definitely be fulfilled.

"Now the LORD had said to Abram...I will make you a great nation...and in you all the families of the earth shall be blessed." Genesis 12:1-3 NKJV

And so it is, there will be people of all nations present in the millennial kingdom and on the renewed earth, enjoying the presence and provision of almighty God, as promised more than 4000 years ago.

The 'saved' of the nations will be just a 'remnant' as it will be for Israel

There are many who believe that the vast majority of mankind will spend eternity with God.

Such a stand borders on universalism. The Bible is definitely not silent on the concept of universalism which implies in the present context there will be an ultimate universal redemption with reconciliation for all mankind with God in the afterlife.

Universalism is definitely not scriptural.

"Does not the potter have power over the clay, from the same lump to make one vessel for honor and another for dishonor? What if God, wanting to show His wrath and to make His power known, endured with much longsuffering the vessels of wrath prepared for destruction, and that He might make known the riches of his glory on the vessels of mercy, which He had prepared beforehand for glory..." Romans 9:21-23 NKJV

The wisest man in the world, i.e. King Solomon spoke the same truth a millennia before the birth of Christ.

"The LORD has made all for Himself, yes, even the wicked for the day of doom." Proverbs 16:4 NKJV

Let's examine a common Scripture reference and review its meaning with the aid of a Greek dictionary.

"For many are called, but few are chosen." Matthew 22:14 NKJV

The Greek base for 'many' in this verse is *hosos* and has been translated to several English words including 'all' or 'whosoever.'

The Greek base for the term 'called' is *kletos* meaning those who have received the invitation to enter the Kingdom of God.

The Greek base for the term 'but' is *alla* meaning 'opposition,' or 'on the contrary.'

The Greek base for the term 'few' is *oligos* meaning 'small' or 'little.'

The Greek base for the term 'chosen' is *ekloge* meaning 'elect' or 'select.'

One might surmise that there is a universal invitation or call to enter the Kingdom of heaven. That's true; however, the above verse indicates that the majority of mankind will reject that invitation or call.

Jesus was equally succinct on the subject in His famous Sermon on the Mount.

"Enter by the narrow gate; for wide is the gate and broad is the way that leads to destruction, and there are many who go in by it. Because narrow is the gate and

difficult is the way which leads to life, and there are few who find it." Matthew 7:13-14 NKJV

Note again the terms 'many' and 'few.' Jesus reaffirmed the doctrine that the majority of mankind will reject redemption.

Shortly thereafter He was asked again about the many and the few.

"Then one said to Him, 'Lord, are there few who are saved?' And He said to them, 'Strive to enter through the narrow gate, for many... will seek to enter and will not be able.'" Luke 13:23-24 NKJV

The 'many' includes those who subscribe to any doctrine that assigns any credit to performance or works to earn entrance to the Kingdom. Such, by default, deny the all sufficient vicarious death of Christ on the Cross. Those who place their entire hope on the Cross define the 'few.'

In addition, the 'few' were chosen and their names written in the Book of Life at the foundation of the world.

Paul further defined the 'few' as the children of promise and the 'many' as those born according to the flesh.

"For...Abraham had two sons: the one by a bondwoman, the other by a freewoman. But he who was of the bondwoman was born according to the flesh, and he of the freewoman through promise...Now we, brethren, as Isaac was, are

children of promise...So then, brethren, we are not children of the bondwoman but of the free." Galatians 4:22-23, 28, 31 NKJV

It should not be surprising that there are those in this age who support universalism because such teaching appeals to the 'many.' The 'many' do not want to be troubled with the sin issue, its consequences, or the one and only 'narrow' remedy.

To satisfy the 'many' is the objective of political correctness which is a millstone for this great nation and sadly, many churches.

Paul also alerted Timothy that such turning away from the truth would take place during the church age, and is in fact happening today.

"For the time will come when they will not endure sound doctrine, but according to their own desires, because they have itching ears, they will heap up for themselves teachers; and they will turn their ears away from the truth, and be turned aside to fables." 2 Timothy 4:3-4 NKJV

The nations will, however, experience universal resurrection

As stated, the term 'universal' implies the whole of a given population, or more simply, 'all.'

While a minority of mankind will be redeemed, all will be resurrected.

Everyone who has ever died will be raised from the grave in the future. The concept of universalism has several profound Biblical applications.

The first significant use of the term 'all' was to quantify the universal consequences of the original sin in the Garden of Eden.

"Therefore, just as through one man sin entered the world, and death through sin, and thus death spread to all men, because all sinned..." Romans 5:12 NKJV

Paul stressed the universality of sin.

"...for all have sinned and fall short of the glory of God..." Romans 3:23 NKJV

Universal sin produces universal consequences.

"For as in Adam all die..." 1 Corinthians 15:22a NKJV

God had announced in the Garden that disobedience to His commands would result in death.

However, since man was created in God's own image, mankind will never cease to be. All will be resurrected from their graves.

"Do not marvel at this; for the hour is coming in which all who are in the graves will hear His voice and come forth – those who have done good, to the resurrection of life, and those who have done evil, to the resurrection of condemnation." John 5:28-29 NKJV

The wording 'those who have done good' does not mean good works or personal efforts; rather it means those who have obeyed Jesus' teachings and believed in Him for redemption and forgiveness of sins. 'Those who have done evil' refers to those who have rejected His teachings and relied on their self-righteousness for salvation. Such are embodied in current day Pharisees, which abound.

Remember Jodi Arias when she thought she would be given the death penalty. She commented that 'death was the ultimate freedom.' How foolish according to the Bible.

The phrase 'resurrection of life' defines the believers of Christ who will be raised in His likeness and spend eternity in His presence. The 'resurrection of condemnation' defines those who will be raised to stand before the great white throne and be condemned to eternal separation and torment.

Therefore, all mankind born after Adam:

1) Will be born with a predisposition to sin
2) Will sin during their lifetime
3) Will return to dust
4) Will be resurrected
5) Will remain forever

Christ was raised from the grave as proof that His propitiation was accepted to appease a holy and righteous God for the sins of repentant mankind. Furthermore He was raised to judge those who rejected His sacrifice.

"...He (God) has appointed a day on which He will judge the world in righteousness by the Man whom He has ordained. He has given assurance of this to all by raising Him from the dead." Acts 17:31 NKJV

Note again the word 'all.' It reiterates that Christ's resurrection was/is/will be known to the whole world, i.e. universal awareness.

Rejecters of Christ will spend eternity in the place prepared for the one who deceived Eve in the Garden and his followers.

"Then He will also say to those on the left hand, 'Depart from Me, you cursed, into the everlasting fire prepared for the devil and his angels...And these will go away into everlasting punishment, but the righteous into eternal life.'" Matthew 25:41, 46 NKJV

This teaching is reaffirmed in the final book of the Bible where the destiny of those who rejected the offer of redemption is described.

"And they were judged, each one according to his works...And anyone not found written in the Book of Life was cast into the lake of fire." Revelation 20:13b, 15 NKJV

Therefore, a small segment of mankind will be redeemed, but all of mankind will be resurrected.

Every individual can choose in which resurrection they will participate and where they will spend eternity.

God's chosen and those that choose redemption are one in the same.

Chapter 12

The Preeminent 'Woman' in the Bible

The Bible tells of many wonderful and godly women that played significant roles in God's plan of redemption for His chosen.

Following is a portion of a Mother's Day poem written for my wife in 2003. Several famous women of the Bible are featured.

The Seed of the woman was God's perfect plan
to conquer the grave with redemption for man.

Yea, Sarah, Rebecca, and Leah, and Ruth
were all in the lineage of Jesus the Truth.

And Tamar was blessed as a mother unwed
as Rahab, Bath-Sheba, and fair Jochebed.

Hagar, Naomi, and Hannah of old
showed love for their children more precious than gold.

*All down through the ages there were many others
delighting Jehovah by serving as mothers.*

*Ah, the love of a mother lasts longer than life
and my children enjoy such a love from my wife.*

The preeminent woman, however, was there in the beginning, even before Eve.

In the book of Proverbs God's attribute of wisdom is personified as a woman evidenced by Solomon referring to wisdom as 'her' and/or 'she.'

Wisdom has been prepared to guide the 'sons of men' who are her delight. Solomon reveals that wisdom was with God in the very beginning when His plan was made for those created in His own image.

"To you, O men, I call, and my voice is to the sons of men...by me kings reign, and rulers decree justice...The LORD possessed me at the beginning of His ways, before His works of old. I have been established from everlasting, from the beginning. Before there was ever an earth...Then I was beside Him as a master craftsman; and I was daily His delight...rejoicing in His inhabited world, and my delight was with the sons of men." Proverbs 8:4, 15, 22-23, 30-31 NKJV

Solomon confirmed that wisdom was with God in the beginning as a master craftsman implementing God's plan. God assigned wisdom to reveal to the 'sons of men' the person and purpose of Himself. Then wisdom and Christ must be one, and so it is.

"...Christ the power of God and the wisdom of God..." I Corinthians 1:24b NASB

"But by His doing you are in Christ Jesus, who became to us wisdom from God, and righteousness and sanctification and redemption." 1 Corinthians 1:30 NASB

Wisdom defined

Wisdom is from the feminine Hebrew noun *chokhmah* meaning 'knowledge,' 'experience,' 'understanding,' 'intelligence,' 'insight,' and 'judgment.' It is always used in a positive sense. Wisdom is of God, not man's perception of truth.

"Wisdom shouts in the street, she lifts her voice in the square; at the head of the noisy streets she cries out; at the entrance of the gates in the city, she utters her sayings..." Proverbs 1:20-21 NASB

Solomon confirmed that God desires man to acquire wisdom, which is offered freely and openly. Man can acquire wisdom if they would submit to wisdom's call; however, most would reject that call. Such rejection would result in disaster.

"Because I called, and you refused; I stretched out my hand, and no one paid attention; and you neglected all my

counsel, and did not want my reproof; I will even laugh at your calamity, I will mock when your dread comes, when your dread comes like a storm." Proverbs 1:24-27 NASB

In the following chapter of Proverbs Solomon again referred to wisdom as 'her.'

"For if you cry for discernment, lift your voice for understanding; if you seek her as silver, and search for her as for hidden treasures; then you will discern the fear of the LORD, and discover the knowledge of God." Proverbs 2:3-5 NASB

Therefore, 'she' (wisdom) provides the knowledge and understanding of God, the very gift of life itself. And it's free for the asking.

The Hebrew word for 'understanding' is very similar to the Greek 'wisdom' with several synonyms including 'discernment' and 'prudence.'

"How blessed is the man who finds wisdom, and the man who gains understanding, for its (her) profit is better than the profit of silver, and its gain than fine gold...and nothing you desire compares with her...she is a tree of life to those who take hold of her..." Proverbs 3:13-15, 18 NASB

What a woman!

Solomon taught his children to embrace wisdom

Solomon pleads with his children to heed his teachings.

"Hear, O sons, the instruction of a father...Acquire wisdom! Acquire understanding! ...Do not forsake her, and she will guard you; love her, and she will watch over you... Take hold of instruction; do not let go. Guard her, for she is your life." Proverbs 4:1, 5-6, 13 NASB

Solomon continuously exhorted his son to grasp and cling to wisdom. He explained that wisdom would protect his son at all times in all places.

"My son, observe the commandment of your father, and do not forsake the teaching of your mother; bind them continually on your heart; tie them around your neck. When you walk about, they will guide you; when you sleep, they will watch over you; and when you awake, they will talk to you."
Proverbs 6:20-22 NASB

The superiority of wisdom

Those who believe the Bible is credible and the source of knowledge and wisdom have a base for understanding and discernment. The Bible has a great deal to say about those who take Biblical teachings lightly. Everyone has the freedom of choice as to view the Bible as credible or not.

Many will reject wisdom's call.

"Wisdom calls aloud outside...'How long, you simple ones, will you love simplicity? For scorners delight in their scorning, and fools hate knowledge.'" Proverbs 1:20a, 22 NKJV

There are three levels of rejection in the above passage. The first level is termed 'simple' which from its Hebrew base means 'seducible' or 'ignorant.' The next level is termed 'scorners.' Scorners mock or deride the truth, and thirdly are 'fools' meaning 'stupid,' 'obstinate,' or 'those who won't listen.'

The Hebrew term for 'knowledge' in the above Scripture means 'insight' and/or 'understanding.'

"...and attaining to all the wealth that comes from the full assurance of understanding, resulting in a true knowledge of God's mystery, that is, Christ Himself, in whom are hidden all the treasures of wisdom and knowledge." Colossians 2:2b-3 NASB

So then, to desire wisdom is to desire the person of Christ. Wisdom is made readily available to those who seek it.

"But if any of you lacks wisdom, let him ask of God, who gives to all men generously..." James 1:5 NASB

And true wisdom will transcend any counterfeit.

"But the wisdom from above is first pure, then peaceable, gentle, reasonable, full of mercy and good fruits, unwavering, without hypocrisy." James 3:17 NASB

Therefore, true wisdom is priceless and readily available. But there will always be those who would rather go it on their own. The Bible also addresses that segment of any population, i.e. the majority.

"Because they hated knowledge, and did not choose the fear of the LORD...They spurned all my reproof. So they shall eat of the fruit of their own way...for the waywardness of the naïve shall kill them, and the complacency of fools shall destroy them." Proverbs 1:29-32 NASB

The redeemed are known by their wisdom

The Apostle Paul had much to say about knowledge and wisdom in his letters.

As he wrote to the Christians in Corinth he stated:

"Yet we do speak wisdom among those who are mature; a wisdom, however, not of this age, nor of the rulers of this age, who are passing away (coming to nothing); but we speak God's wisdom in a mystery, the hidden wisdom, which God predestined before the ages to our glory; the wisdom which none of the rulers of this age has understood..." 1 Corinthians 2:6-8 NASB

The Greek base for wisdom in this passage describes insight imparted from God to the believer. He firmly declares that man's wisdom exercised by the rulers of this age will certainly fail.

True wisdom granted by God to His chosen was a mystery hidden since before time began. Worldly wisdom is vanity and will profit nothing.

Paul goes on to explain that worldly wisdom vs. the things of God is mutually exclusive.

"But the natural man does not receive the things of the Spirit of God, for they are foolishness to him; nor can he know them, because they are spiritually discerned." 1 Corinthians 2:14 NKJV

The Greek for 'know' in the above verse means 'to perceive or understand.'

The wisdom of God is not even available to the natural man, i.e. one who does not possess the Spirit of God. Only God's Spirit can quicken the mind to understand spiritual things, or true wisdom.

Paul reemphasized this truth in his second letter to the Christians in Corinth.

"For our proud confidence is this, the testimony of our conscience, that in holiness and godly sincerity, not

in fleshly wisdom...we have conducted ourselves in the world." 2 Corinthians 1:12 NASB

Worldly, or fleshly wisdom, is from the Greek *agnoeo* and means to be in 'ignorance, lacking discernment.' It is based on a worldly perspective. Again, worldly wisdom is totally incompatible with God's wisdom which He imparts to His chosen.

The world wants to reason their surroundings and circumstances while God's chosen accept his surroundings and circumstances by faith without question.

"Who among you is wise and understanding? Let him show by his good behavior his deeds in the gentleness of wisdom. But if you have bitter jealousy and selfish ambition in your heart, do not be arrogant and so lie against the truth. This wisdom is not that which comes down from above, but is earthly...For where jealousy and selfish ambition exist, there is disorder and every evil thing." James 3:13-16 NASB

The Greek for 'wise' in the first sentence of this passage means 'wisdom relative to divine truths,' 'enlightenment,' and 'pure of heart.' The meaning of 'understanding' in the present context means 'to know thoroughly and expertly.'

But worldly wisdom exhibited by natural man is self-seeking. It is of the earth and not of God. It produces confusion and further alienates one from God. It is totally contrary to the truth.

A promise for those who genuinely seek wisdom

"But he who listens to me shall live securely, and shall be at ease from the dread of evil." Proverbs 1:33 NASB

The Hebrew for 'evil' in the above passage has several synonyms including 'disaster,' 'adversity,' 'distress,' or 'calamity.'

Wisdom, embodied in Christ is sought and embraced by God's chosen, i.e. the redeemed remnant.

Thought for today

Is America dwelling safely now, and is she living securely without the fear of evil?

The benchmark for God's standard of justice and definition of righteousness has not changed through the ages, nor will it change. One of God's attributes is His immutability.

Those who believe America has rejected wisdom would also believe those responsible for decision making at the national level are content to be simpletons, scorners, or fools.

The consequences of this great nation rejecting wisdom are becoming more obvious each day.

Only fools would reject that which is superior and free.

Chapter 13

The 'Other Woman'

Solomon tells of another 'woman' quite the opposite of wisdom. She is equally as enthusiastic as wisdom with her appeal, but her message, while flattering, appeals to the natural instincts of the naïve, mockers, and fools.

It all began for the 'other woman' when the curse was pronounced on the serpent in the garden.

"And I will put enmity between you and the woman, and between your seed and her Seed..." Genesis 3:15 NKJV

Therefore, there must be a mother involved in order to produce evil seed. And so it was and will be; the mother who produced evil seed is active throughout the Bible up to the 19th chapter of the book of Revelation where she is called 'the great harlot.'

It is interesting to note that Solomon explains that embracing wisdom is the best way to resist the allures of the other woman.

"When wisdom enters your heart, and knowledge is pleasant to your soul, discretion will preserve you; understanding will keep you, to deliver you from the way of evil...to deliver you from the immoral woman, from the seductress who flatters with her words...for her house leads down to death, and her paths to the dead..." Proverbs 2:10-12a, 16, 18 NKJV

The immoral woman speaks to itching ears. The Hebrew for 'immoral' is *zur* with several meanings including 'to be strange,' or 'to be adulterous.' A 'strange' woman in Hebrew in the present context means a woman who is not a man's own wife and one who initiates illicit sexual relations. And the Hebrew term for 'seductress' means to 'lead astray' and/or 'deceive.'

Whereas wisdom leads to life, the other woman leads to death.

Solomon warns his son to be on guard.

"My son, give attention to my wisdom...for the lips of an adulteress drip honey, and smoother than oil is her speech; but in the end she is bitter as wormwood..." Proverbs 5:1a, 3-4a NASB

The above word 'smoother' in Hebrew is synonymous with 'flatter.'

Solomon warns his son to resist temptation by not wandering close to the immoral woman's house. The consequences are too great.

"Keep your way far from her, and do not go near the door of her house...for why should you, my son, be exhilarated with an adulteress and embrace the bosom of a foreigner (seductress)?" Proverbs 5:8, 20 NASB

Introduction to harlotry

Solomon's advice advances from seduction to harlotry. The temptation would turn to illicit action.

"Do not desire her beauty in your heart, nor let her catch you with her eyelids, for on account of a harlot one is reduced to a loaf of bread, and an adulteress hunts for the precious life." Proverbs 6:25-26 NASB

The harlot is the means by which the evil one deceives man. The devil appeals to the natural instincts of man, enticing him to reject wisdom. It personifies the battle between good and evil.

The Hebrew for harlot is very important with multiple implications. The term means generally 'illicit sexual activity usually applicable to women.' That is significant inasmuch as Israel is said to be betrothed to God, so only the woman could be involved in such activity.

And, depending on specific context, the word can be used figuratively to mean 'illegal contact between Israel and other nations.' Israel's harlotry is a significant transgression throughout their history.

Solomon then presents a vivid example of how a naïve man without wisdom could be seduced. He begins by telling how a crafty, or cunning, harlot seeks her victims. The plot is narrated by an observer looking out his window.

"For at the window of my house I looked through my lattice, and saw among the simple, I perceived among the youths, a young man devoid of understanding, passing along the street near her corner; and he took the path to her house...and there a woman met him with the attire of a harlot, and a crafty heart." Proverbs 7:6-8, 10 NKJV

Recall the Hebrew for 'understanding' is synonymous with 'wisdom.'

The word 'crafty' in the above is 'subtle' in the KJV and is the same word used to describe the serpent in Genesis.

"Now the serpent was more crafty (cunning, subtle, deceitful) than any beast of the field which the LORD God had made..." Genesis 3:1 NASB

The harlot told the naïve one that she had prepared for him that which appeals to the senses.

"I have spread my couch with coverings, with colored linens of Egypt. I have sprinkled my bed with myrrh, aloes and cinnamon...let us delight ourselves with caresses." Proverbs 7:16-18 NASB

The unsuspecting victim was entrapped.

"With her many persuasions she entices him; with her flattering lips she seduces him. Suddenly he follows her, as an ox goes to the slaughter, or as one in fetters to the discipline of a fool, until an arrow pierces through his liver; as a bird hastens to the snare, so he does not know that it will cost him his life." Proverbs 7:21-23 NASB

The seductress told the victim that their illicit activities were safe, inasmuch as her husband was on a long journey.

"For my husband is not at home; he has gone on a long journey...and will come home on the appointed day." Proverbs 7:19-20 NKJV

Notice the prophetic implications of the above.

"But of that day or hour no one knows, not even the angels in heaven, nor the Son, but the Father alone. Take heed, keep on the alert; for you do not know when the appointed time is. It is like a man, away on a journey, who upon leaving his house...Therefore, be on the alert – for you do not know when the master of the house is coming, whether in the evening, at midnight, at cockcrowing, or in the morning..." Mark 13:32-35 NASB

The 'strange' or 'immoral' woman that Solomon spoke of is also an imposter. She offers something for temporal advantage in place of the truth. The one who takes her bait has chosen death.

"The woman of folly is boisterous, she is naïve, and knows nothing. And she sits at the doorway of her house, on a seat by the high places of the city, calling to those who pass by, who are making their paths straight: 'Whoever is naïve, let him turn in here,' and to him who lacks understanding she says, 'stolen water is sweet; and bread eaten in secret is pleasant.' But he does not know that the dead are there, that her guests are in the depths of Sheol." Proverbs 9:13-18 NASB

And so it is every man is confronted by two women. Both of them openly seek to share their offerings. One of them offers life and the other offers death. One represents the Seed of the woman who would destroy the evil one, and the other is the seed of the evil one who would be destroyed. Such, once again, defines the two categories of all mankind.

Israel, the betrothed of God, plays the harlot

The prophets were not silent on the subject of Israel's harlotry, or spiritual adultery.

God instructed the prophet Hosea to marry Gomer who would commit harlotry. Her harlotry was to portray Israel's spiritual adultery to her betrothed, i.e. God.

"When the LORD first spoke through Hosea, the LORD said to Hosea, 'Go, take to yourself a wife of harlotry; and have children of harlotry; for the land commits flagrant harlotry, forsaking the LORD.'" Hosea 1:2 NASB

The Hebrew for harlotry in the present context relates to business dealings with foreigners.

Speaking of their children, Hosea said:

"For their mother has played the harlot; she who conceived them has acted shamefully, for she said, 'I will go after my lovers, who give me my bread and my water, my wool and my flax, my oil and my drink.'" Hosea 2:5 NASB

Israel's true provider

Gomer (as Israel) thought other nations, i.e. her lovers, had provided for her instead of her betrothed husband Hosea, or God. God in turn prevented her lovers to provide for her so she would return to her real husband.

"Therefore, behold, I will hedge up her way with thorns, and I will build a wall against her so that she cannot find her paths. And she will pursue her lovers, but she will not overtake them; and she will seek them but will not find them. Then she will say, 'I will go back to my first husband, for it was better for me then than now!'" Hosea 2:6-7 NASB

Gomer hadn't realized that her husband had provided for her all along. God in His longsuffering led her step by step back to His provision and protection.

God will forgive Israel's harlotry

God then confirmed His eternal relationship with His betrothed, regardless of what she had done.

"And I will betroth you to Me forever; Yes, I will betroth you to Me in righteousness and in justice, in lovingkindness and in compassion, and I will betroth you to Me in faithfulness. Then you will know the LORD." Hosea 2:19-20 NASB

God then told Hosea to take Gomer back as his wife.

"Then the LORD said to me, 'Go again, love a woman who is loved by her husband, yet an adulteress, even as the LORD loves the sons of Israel, though they turn to other gods...'" Hosea 3:1 NASB

Hosea then confirmed that his relationship with Gomer portrayed God's love for Israel. God's promises to Abraham and his descendants are eternal and immutable. After many years of dispersion and chastisement, Israel will return to their provider and God.

"Afterward the sons of Israel will return and seek the LORD their God and David their king; and they will come

trembling to the LORD and to His goodness in the last days." Hosea 3:5 NASB

Hosea's story is another great illustration of history written in advance for an example and benefit for all other nations. The other nations had best be aligning themselves with God's pre-written plan.

America has no excuse, inasmuch as God has revealed Himself and His purpose to all nations.

Israel's capital city...the epitome of harlotry

"How the faithful city has become a harlot, she who was full of justice! Righteousness once lodged in her, but now murderers. Our silver has become dross, your drink diluted with water. Your rulers are rebels, and companions of thieves, every one loves a bribe, and chases after rewards..." Isaiah 1:21-23 NASB

The city that had been blessed with everything had turned against their Provider. The prophet Ezekiel supplied much more detail about Jerusalem's unfaithfulness.

"I also clothed you with...fine linen and covered you with silk. And I adorned you with ornaments ...and a beautiful crown on your head Thus you were adorned with gold and silver, and your dress was of fine linen, silk, and embroidered cloth. You ate fine flour, honey, and oil; so you were exceedingly beautiful and advanced to royalty.

Then your fame went forth among the nations on account of your beauty for it was perfect because of My splendor which I bestowed on you,' declares the Lord God." Ezekiel 16:10-14 NASB

Note that everything Jerusalem had had been given to her by God, i.e. "…I bestowed on you." She was famous among all the nations because of God's blessings.

The Psalmist called Jerusalem 'the joy of the whole earth' and 'the city of the great King.'

Jerusalem was blessed with everything; however, the very first word in the following verse in the Ezekiel passage is 'but.'

"But you trusted in your beauty and played the harlot because of your fame, and you poured out your harlotries on every passer-by who might be willing." Ezekiel 16:15 NASB

Jerusalem used what God had provided to make idols and decorate places of idol worship.

"And you took some of your clothes, made for yourself high places…and played the harlot on them…You also took your beautiful jewels made of My gold and of My silver, which I had given you, and made for yourself male images…" Ezekiel 16:16-17 NASB

Their harlotry continued to worsen. Jerusalem made covenants with nations that were at enmity with God for their treatment of Israel including Egypt, the Philistines, the Assyrians, and even Chaldea.

Jerusalem shunned God's provision and protection and sought provision and protection from others. They were seeking something they already had. They thought they could do better with their own plan and strategy.

"'How languishing (degenerate) is your heart,' declares the Lord God, 'while you do all these things, the actions of a bold-faced harlot.'" Ezekiel 16:30 NASB

Worse than the typical harlot

It seems that Jerusalem's harlotry was insatiable. God tells them that they were even worse than a harlot.

"When you built your shrine at the beginning of every street and made your high place in every square, in disdaining money, you were not like a harlot...Men give gifts to all harlots, but you give your gifts to all your lovers to bribe them to come to you from every direction for your harlotries. Thus you are different from those women in your harlotries, in that no one plays the harlot as you do, because you give money and no money is given you; thus you are different (opposite)." Ezekiel 16:31, 33-34 NASB

Jerusalem was worse than a traditional harlot because instead of taking money for her harlotry, she paid her lovers. She was just the opposite of a traditional harlot. She paid tribute to enemy nations and gave them the provisions God had given to her.

In summary, Jerusalem trusted in her own beauty, i.e. she did not acknowledge the fact that all she had was given to her. She used what had been given to her to support idols. She killed babies that God called His own. She sought out protection from enemy nations and paid them tribute.

Implications for today

What Jerusalem did brings to mind some of the issues prevalent in America today. This great nation touts American Exceptionalism and takes credit for everything she has.

America supports and funds activities that are absolutely counter to God's standard of righteousness. America kills hundreds of thousands of babies yearly, and lastly America gives foreign aid to enemy nations.

Jerusalem was in the past, is presently, and will in the future be judged for her harlotry, as God did, and will again, deliver her to and from her enemies.

"Thus says the Lord God, 'Because your lewdness was poured out...through your harlotries with your lovers and

with all your detestable idols, and because of the blood of your sons...therefore, behold, I shall gather all your lovers with whom you took pleasure, even all those whom you loved and all those whom you hated. So I shall gather them against you from every direction and expose your nakedness to them...'" Ezekiel 16:36-37 NASB

Will America fare any better?

The New Testament likewise labels this current generation as adulterous and self seeking.

"You adulteresses, do you not know that friendship with the world is hostility toward God? Therefore whoever wishes to be a friend of the world makes himself an enemy of God." James 4:4 NASB

The Greek for 'adulteresses' means 'those who yield themselves to their own lusts.' Synonymous characteristics include infidelity, faithless, and idolatrous. The word can be used interchangeably with 'harlot' from the Greek *porne* which includes illicit activity of any kind, married or unmarried.

Harlotry will continue to the end of this age.

"...and I saw a woman sitting on a scarlet beast, full of blasphemous names...the woman was clothed in purple and scarlet, and adorned with gold and precious stones and pearls, having in her hand a gold cup full of abominations

and of the unclean things of her immorality (fornication)."
Revelation 17:3-4 NASB

The identification of the great harlot and her demise

Near the end of the future great tribulation period the ultimate harlot of all ages is revealed and explained.

"Then one of the seven angels who had the seven bowls came and talked with me, saying to me, 'Come, I will show you the judgment of the great harlot who sits on many waters, with whom the kings of the earth committed fornication...'" Revelation 17:1-2 NKJV

As mentioned the Greek for 'harlot,' is *porne*. Its basic meaning in the above context is 'to sell,' i.e. 'the activities of a merchant.' Babylon is called the great harlot, inasmuch as it is the seat of idolatry.

Therefore, *porne* is also synonymous with the Greek *piprasko* meaning 'to traffic or merchandise,' particularly beyond the sea in other lands. Similar phraseology includes 'engaging in business, trade.'

The term 'fornication' in the above is from the Greek *porkios* which symbolically means 'the forsaking of the true God in order to worship idols.' Inasmuch as God was symbolically betrothed to Israel and Christ is the bridegroom of the church, any idolatry is unfaithfulness, i.e. spiritual adultery toward God.

Harlotry, or spiritual adultery, will accelerate to the point of no return

"...and those who dwell on the earth were made drunk with the wine of her immorality (fornication)." Revelation 17:2b NASB

The term 'drunk' in the above is from the Greek *methuo* which means in the present context 'never having enough to satisfy.'

"And upon her forehead a name was written, mystery, 'BABYLON THE GREAT, THE MOTHER OF HARLOTS AND OF THE ABOMINATIONS OF THE EARTH.'" Revelation 17:5 NASB

The meaning of 'mystery' in the above 'denotes a spiritual truth couched under an external representation or similitude and concealed or hidden, thereby, unless some explanation is given in their respective context.'

In other words a mystery was/is a part of God's eternal plan that would be revealed in His timing. Such a mystery would be manifested externally but would not be understood until explained. Many of Jesus' parables were mysteries until He explained their meaning to His disciples.

The term 'Babylon' in the above is a symbolic name for heathen Rome and means in essence 'evil.' It equates metaphorically ancient Babylon with the final world's idolatry and harlotry.

The term 'mother' is a figurative term meaning 'the parent or source of wickedness and abominations.' The seed of the enemy mentioned in the early chapters of Genesis would come through 'the mother of harlots.'

"And I will put enmity between...your seed and her Seed..." Genesis 3:15 NKJV

And lastly, the word 'abomination' in the above means 'impure idol worship' which would ultimately be associated with the anti-Christ spoken of by Daniel the prophet.

The Apostle John noted that the mother of harlots was drunk.

Not only was the great harlot drunk with the wine of her fornication, she was drunk with the blood of the saints. She just couldn't get enough of her harlotry, i.e. spiritual adultery or idolatry, and she also had an insatiable appetite for the blood of God's people.

"And the woman whom you saw is the great city, which reigns over the kings of the earth." Revelation 17:18 NASB

The great harlot has universal implications

Her activities are further described.

"For all the nations have drunk of the wine of the wrath of her fornication, the kings of the earth have committed fornication with her, and the merchants of the earth

have become rich through the abundance of her luxury."
Revelation 18:3 NKJV

This commercial aspect of her activities should not be surprising, inasmuch as 'harlot' is related to 'sell,' or 'to traffic in merchandise.' Her demise is sure.

Recall the ancient King of Tyre and God's proclamation to him via the Prophet Ezekiel.

"And you, son of man (Ezekiel), take up a lamentation over Tyre; and say to Tyre, who dwells at the entrance to the sea, merchant of the peoples to many coastlands... 'By your wisdom and understanding you have acquired riches for yourself, and have acquired gold and silver for your treasuries. By your great wisdom, by your trade you have increased your riches, and your heart is lifted up because of your riches...'" Ezekiel 27:2-3, 28:4-5 NASB

The great harlot who committed spiritual adultery against her God by departing from His precepts and embracing transitory riches is dealt with mightily.

"And a strong angel took up a stone like a great millstone and threw it into the sea, saying, 'Thus will Babylon, the great city, be thrown down with violence, and will not be found any longer.'" Revelation 18:21 NASB

Such was all part of God's eternal plan. The prophet Jeremiah spoke of Babylon, past and future, approximately six centuries before the birth of Christ.

"Babylon has been a golden cup in the hand of the LORD, intoxicating all the earth. The nations have drunk of her wine; therefore the nations are going mad. Suddenly Babylon has fallen and been broken..." Jeremiah 51:7-8a NASB

The cup in the LORD's hand exemplifies God's sovereignty. All nations would partake of the harlot's offerings. Babylon fell to the Medes and Persians after Judah's 70 year captivity, and the present Babylon will fall suddenly and completely in the future.

God will also judge all nations that would drink from the golden cup.

"For thus the LORD, the God of Israel, says to me, 'Take this cup of the wine of wrath from My hand, and cause all the nations, to whom I send you, to drink it. And they shall drink and stagger and go mad because of the sword that I will send among them.'" Jeremiah 25:15-16 NASB

The cities and nations identified to drink of the cup begin with Jerusalem and the cities of Judah, Egypt, Uz, Philistines, Ashkelon, Gaza, Ekron, Ashdod, Edom, Moab, Ammon, Tyre, all the kings of Sidon, Dedan, Tema, Buz, all the kings of Arabia, all the kings of Zimri, all the kings of Elam, and all the kings of the Medes, all the kings of the north…and all the kingdoms of the world which are on the face of the earth. Jeremiah's instructions had both short and long-range implications.

Interestingly, the final ten nation federation in the final seventh world kingdom will rise up and violently destroy the harlot.

"Then he (angel) said to me (John), 'The waters which you saw where the harlot sits, are peoples and multitudes and nations and tongues. And the ten horns which you saw, and the beast, these will hate the harlot and will make her desolate and naked, and will eat her flesh and will burn her up with fire. For God has put it in their hearts to execute His purpose by having a common purpose, and by giving their kingdom to the beast, until the words of God should be fulfilled.'" Revelation 17:15-17 NASB

The great harlot, the object of universal spiritual adultery, affects all nations on the earth. The ten nations of the final world kingdom will rise up and destroy the harlot according to God's plan determined from the foundation of the world. At that time the final confederation will join together as one and accept the anti-Christ as their leader.

It is believed that the harlot represents the 'lust of the flesh, the lust of the eyes, and the pride of life' vs. God's eternal rewards.

Could it be that the great harlot is epitomized by western civilization?

And if so, who in the 'world' would want to destroy such a progressive ideology?

Chapter 14

Shedding Innocent Blood

The Apostle John saw that the mother of harlots who reigned over the kings of the earth was drunk also with blood.

"And I saw the woman drunk with the blood of the saints, and with the blood of the witnesses (martyrs) of Jesus." Revelation 17:6 NASB

The Greek word for 'blood' in this verse is *haima* which means 'life taken away by force.'

"And in her was found the blood of prophets and of saints and of all who have been slain on the earth." Revelation 18:24 NASB

The consequences of shedding innocent man's blood by man

As mentioned earlier it was/is a capital offense for a man to spill the blood of an innocent human, inasmuch as man is created in the very image of God.

Israel, however, shed much blood during their history. This sin was as abominable as their idolatry in God's eyes.

Numerous times in the Old Testament, God condemned Israel and her capital city Jerusalem for their bloodshed and idolatry.

"And you (Ezekiel) shall say, ' thus says the Lord God... You have become guilty by the blood which you have shed, and defiled by your idols which you have made.'" Ezekiel 22:3-4 NASB

The killing of infants

The shedding of innocent blood by Israel included the killing of her children by offering them to false gods. Such a thing was an abomination to God.

"They even sacrificed their sons and their daughters to the demons, and shed innocent blood, the blood of their sons and their daughters, whom they sacrificed to the idols of Canaan; and the land was polluted with the blood...and played the harlot in their deeds." Psalm 106:37-39 NASB

God said that such an abomination never entered His mind.

"And they built the high places of Baal that are in the valley of Ben-hinnom to cause their sons and their daughters to pass through the fire to Molech, which I had not commanded them or had it entered My mind that

they should do this abomination, to cause Judah to sin." Jeremiah 32:35 NASB

Such departure from the word of God was not only idolatry, but also spiritual adultery, or harlotry.

"Moreover, you took your sons and daughters whom you had borne to Me, and you sacrificed them to idols to be devoured. Were your harlotries so small a matter? You slaughtered My children, and offered them up to idols by causing them to pass through the fire." Ezekiel 16:20-21 NASB

Some might surmise in today's world that such an abomination compares with the present practice of legalized abortion. Others would argue that a fetus does not become a child until the child is born.

The Bible very clearly addresses the issue. Recall when Isaac's wife Rebekah was with child.

"And Isaac prayed to the LORD on behalf of his wife, because she was barren; and the LORD answered him and Rebekah his wife conceived. But the children struggled together within her...when her days to be delivered were fulfilled, behold, there were twins in her womb." Genesis 25:21-22a, 24 NASB

The Hebrew base for 'children' in the above scripture is *Ben* defined as a 'son, child, boy, or young one.' And the Hebrew base for 'womb' is *Beten* meaning 'belly,' 'within,' or 'inmost part.' In other words, Rebekah had two living sons within her body. One of those sons was subsequently named Jacob who was later renamed 'Israel.'

The Apostle Paul confirmed the identity and significance of unborn children.

"...there was Rebekah also, when she had conceived twins by one man, our father Isaac; for though the twins were not yet born, and had not done anything good or bad, in order that God's purpose according to His choice might stand, not because of works, but because of Him who calls, it was said to her, 'THE OLDER WILL SERVE THE YOUNGER.' Just as it is written, 'JACOB I LOVED, BUT ESAU I HATED.'" Romans 9:10-13 NASB

God had called the brothers by name and had pre-written their part in His master plan devised before the foundation of the world. The Bible succinctly states His calling for the brothers was announced while they were 'not yet being born.'

There is a segment in America today that has gone beyond the killing of innocent unborn children.

Planned Parenthood shocked the nation in 2015 when it was revealed that their services include not only the slaughter of the unborn but harvesting parts of their bodies for profit.

King David addressed the significance of newly conceived children within their mother's womb as he attempted to express the majesty and sovereignty of God.

"My frame was not hidden from You, when I was made in secret...Your eyes saw my substance, being yet unformed. And in Your book they all were written, the days fashioned for me, when as yet there were none of them." Psalm 139:15-16 NKJV

David confirms that God's purpose for His chosen was set in ages past and their days determined and outlined before they were even formed in their mother's womb. Their days are already numbered and recorded in the Book of Life.

Roe v. Wade has legally allowed the murder of approximately 57 million children.

Such a law brings to mind the words of Jesus to the Pharisees.

"Why do you also transgress the commandment of God because of your tradition? ...Thus you have made the commandment of God of no effect by your tradition." Matthew 15:3, 6 NKJV

A child is a child whether running across the room into a parent's protective arms or resting in peace within their mother's protective womb awaiting birth.

The guilt and hypocrisy of the Pharisees

During Jesus' time on earth He confronted the Pharisees with their hypocrisy when they told Jesus that if they had lived in the days of their fathers, they would not have been partakers in shedding blood of the prophets.

Jesus soundly denounced them and called them sons of those who murdered the prophets, inasmuch as they wanted to kill Him.

"Therefore, behold, I am sending you prophets and wise men and scribes; some of them you will kill and crucify, and some of them you will scourge in your synagogues, and persecute from city to city, that upon you may fall the guilt of all the righteous blood shed on earth, from the blood of righteous Abel..." Matthew 23:34-35 NASB

During the great tribulation the Apostle John hears an angel confirm Jesus' justice in His judgments.

"...for they poured out the blood of saints and prophets and Thou hast given them blood to drink. They deserve it." Revelation 16:6 NASB

When Christ returns to complete the redemption process, He will justifiably shed much blood of His enemies.

A song of retribution

During the celebration of Independence Day, many patriotic songs are sung with great exuberance. One of the most popular is the *Battle Hymn of the Republic*. The words of this powerful song link the historical American Civil War with the great war of the future.

"Mine eyes have seen the glory of the coming of the Lord;

He is trampling out the vintage where the grapes of wrath are stored;

He hath loosed the fateful lightning of His terrible swift sword:

His truth is marching on."

The Biblical background for this great song is found throughout the scriptures ending in the Book of Revelation. References are found as far back as the 9th century BC.

One of the great truths of the Bible is that Christ will return to earth and judge the nations, in addition to Israel.

"Draw near, O nations, to hear; and listen, O peoples! ...For the LORD's indignation is against all the nations...The sword of the LORD is filled with blood...For the LORD has a day of vengeance..." Isaiah 34:1, 2, 6, 8 NASB

The above passage confirms that Christ will, on the appointed day, return to earth and deal with the nations. The term 'indignation' signifies the 'righteous anger of Jehovah.'

Isaiah then tells that the LORD will return with a sword that will be filled with blood. The term 'vengeance' means 'revenge,' 'retaliation,' and/or 'punishment.' Vengeance belongs solely to God. And then note that God's indignation is against all nations.

Isaiah subsequently reaffirms his message in more detail.

"Why is Your apparel red, and Your garments like the one who treads in the wine press?... 'I have trodden the wine trough alone...and trampled them in My wrath; and their life blood is sprinkled on My garments, and I stained all My raiment. For the day of vengeance was in My heart, and My year of redemption has come.'" Isaiah 63:2-4 NASB

Isaiah again speaks of the LORD's anger in the day of vengeance. Notice that he also speaks of the LORD's garments sprinkled with blood and likens that with the results of one who treads in the winepress.

Even several centuries before Isaiah, the Prophet Joel spoke of the same future events using similar descriptive language.

"Let the nations be aroused and come up to the valley of Jehoshaphat, for there I will sit to judge all the surrounding nations. Put in the sickle, for the harvest is ripe...for the winepress is full; the vats overflow, for their wickedness is great." Joel 3:12-13 NASB

Joel used the metaphor of reaping with a sickle. The sickle was used when the crop was ready for harvest. He also used metaphoric language of the fullness of the winepress meaning the height of the wickedness of the nations.

Joel wrote nearly three millennia ago. The words of Isaiah and Joel are summarized by the Apostle John as he wrote of future events which gave birth to the words of the Battle Hymn of the Republic.

"And another angel...called with a loud voice to him who had the sharp sickle, saying, 'Put in your sharp sickle, and gather the clusters from the vine of the earth, because her grapes are ripe.' And the angel swung his sickle to the earth, and gathered the clusters from the vine of the earth, and threw them into the great wine press of the wrath of God. And the wine press was trodden outside the city, and blood came out from the wine press..." Revelation 14:18-20 NASB

John then confirmed the words of Isaiah and Joel. The returning King would judge the nations resulting in an extremely bloody war.

The power of His sword is His spoken word. Christ personally will execute God's righteous judgment on the nations and then will rule them with a rod of iron.

"And I saw heaven opened; and behold, a white horse, and He who sat upon it is called Faithful and True; and in righteousness He judges and wages war...And He is clothed with a robe dipped in blood...and from His mouth comes a sharp sword, so that with it He may smite the nations...

He treads the wine press of the fierce wrath of God, the Almighty." Revelation 19:11, 13, 15 NASB

The retribution on those who shed innocent blood can be traced back to Jacob's prophecy relative to his son Judah.

"...Your hand shall be on the neck of your enemies... Judah is a lion's whelp; from the prey, my son, you have gone up. He couches, he lies down as a lion, and as a lion, who dares rouse him up? He washes his garments in wine, and his robes in the blood of grapes." Genesis 49:8-9 NASB

Glory, Glory, Hallelujah! His truth is marching on!

Chapter 15

The Serpent and His Seed

Before the creation of man, Lucifer son of the morning was the highest of God's creations. But pride entered his heart and he wasn't satisfied to be submissive to his Creator. His aspirations are recorded by the prophet Isaiah.

"...I will raise my throne above the stars of God...I will make myself like the Most High." Isaiah 14:13-14 NASB

Pride takes place when a created being uses the term 'I will' and attributes to one's own power that which God has provided.

The Isaiah passage above was simultaneously describing the mindset of Babylon's King Nebuchadnezzar who was a puppet of Satan who was in turn a puppet of the One who created him.

Recall Nebuchadnezzar also attributed what God had given him to his own efforts as did his puppeteer, i.e. Satan.

"The king (Nebuchadnezzar) reflected and said, 'Is this not Babylon the great, which I myself have built as a royal residence by the might of my power and for the glory of my majesty?'" Daniel 4:30 NASB

Recall further that Daniel had interpreted a previous dream for Nebuchadnezzar which had revealed that because of his pride he was to be reduced to a grass eating beast of the field for seven years.

"While the word was in the king's mouth, a voice came from heaven, saying, 'King Nebuchadnezzar, to you it is declared: sovereignty has been removed from you, and you will be driven away from mankind...You will be given grass to eat like cattle...until you recognize that the Most High is ruler over the realm of mankind, and bestows it on whomever He wishes.'" Daniel 4:31-32 NASB

After Satan's humiliating loss evidenced by the Babylonian Kingdom being taken from Nebuchadnezzar and also the humiliating removal of the king of Tyre who was also energized by Satan, one might have assumed that he would have rethought using the words 'I will.' Such was/is not the case.

Another appointed world leader and pride

Remember the Assyrian king Sennacherib who exhibited great pride centuries before Nebuchadnezzar; he also touted his kingdom and power.

"With my many chariots I came up to the heights of the mountains, to the remotest part of Lebanon...I dug wells and drank foreign waters, and with the sole of my feet I dried up all the rivers of Egypt." 2 Kings 19:23-24 NASB

He was boasting about his accomplishments and threatening Judah's King Hezekiah not to trust in Israel's God. Sennacherib was in fact mocking Israel's God. He reminded Hezekiah of all his victories and conquests. Then God sent word to Hezekiah through Isaiah.

"This is the word that the LORD has spoken against him: ... 'The virgin daughter of Zion; she has despised you and mocked you... Whom have you reproached and blasphemed? And against whom have you raised your voice, and haughtily lifted up your eyes? Against the Holy One of Israel!'" 2 Kings 19:21-22 NASB

God's proclamation against Sennacherib:

"Because of your raging against Me, and because your arrogance has come up to My ears, therefore I will put My hook in your nose, and My bridle in your lips, and I will turn you back by the way which you came." Isaiah 37:29 NASB

Sennacherib's humiliating defeat:

"Then the angel of the LORD went out, and struck 185,000 in the camp of the Assyrians; and when men arose early in the morning, behold, all of these were dead. So

Sennacherib, king of Assyria, departed and returned home..." 2 Kings 19:36-37 NASB

Such pride was also illustrated in the New Testament. Recall Pilate's statement to Jesus while interrogating Him.

"*...Do You not know that I have authority (power) to release You, and I have authority to crucify You?*" John 19:10 NASB

Jesus' authoritative response to Pilate:

"*You would have no authority over Me, unless it had been given you from above...*" John 19:11 NASB

Thus it is plainly seen that all power or authority claimed by any of God's creations has been given or granted from above to accomplish God's purpose. It is absolute folly to claim such power has been achieved by one's own efforts.

Ultimate pride

Recall the early days of Jesus' ministry.

"*Then Jesus was led up by the Spirit into the wilderness to be tempted by the devil.*" Matthew 4:1 NASB

It is important to begin by noting that Jesus was led by the Spirit, i.e. God the Father had orchestrated the entire experience of His Son being tempted (tested).

"...the devil...showed Him all the kingdoms of the world, and their glory; and he said to Him, 'All these things will I give You, if You fall down and worship me.'" Matthew 4:8-9 NASB

Of course Jesus replied that only the Lord God should be worshipped and served.

Satan was well aware that what he offered Jesus had been given to him as part of God's master plan. Satan has no power to do anything that God hasn't preordained.

Luke recorded that fact as he recounted the testing of Jesus.

"And the devil said to Him, 'I will give You all the domain and its glory; for it has been handed over to me, and I give it to whomever I wish.'" Luke 4:6 NASB

It all goes back to God's powerful 'I will' in Genesis.

"And I will put enmity between you and the woman, and between your seed and her Seed..." Genesis 3:15 NKJV

Pride before the fall

Following the church age, which is coming to a close, Satan will exalt his granted power more than any time in world history. During the great tribulation Satan will personally energize the future anti-Christ.

"...and the man of lawlessness is revealed, the son of destruction, who opposes and exalts himself above every so-called god or object of worship, so that he takes his seat in the temple of God, displaying himself as being God." 2 Thessalonians 2:3-4 NASB

Paul is describing what Daniel referred to more than 500 years before the birth of Christ, i.e. "And on the wing of abominations shall be one who makes desolate..."

And Jesus confirmed Daniel's prophecy as He was describing future history to His disciples:

"Therefore when you see the ABOMINATION OF DESOLATION which was spoken of through Daniel the prophet, standing in the holy place..." Matthew 24:15 NASB

Satan's 'I wills' will in God's timing become 'I lost' when he finds himself being tormented in the lake of fire 'day and night forever and ever.'

Only God has the right and authority to say "I will."

Not much has changed

In that context it is interesting to note several relevant statements made by President Obama in his 2014 State of the Union address.

"As commander in chief, I have used force when needed...and I will never hesitate to do so as long as I hold this office."

"And as chief executive...I will issue an executive order ..."

"I will use my authority to..."

"So wherever and whenever I can take steps without legislation...that's what I am going to do."

"...I'll act on my own..."

Will he do better than Sennacherib, Nebuchadnezzar, or Pilate?

Seed of the serpent

Just as the Seed of the woman can be traced throughout history which ultimately culminated in the God/Man Jesus Christ, the seed of the serpent can also be found and identified in the Scriptures.

Recall the curse pronounced on the serpent after he had deceived Eve.

*"And I will put enmity...between **your seed** and her Seed..."* Genesis 3:15 NKJV (emphasis added)

God will highlight the absolute opposition between His Son and the serpent throughout the ages. The two lead the battle between good and evil; the redeemed and those that aren't.

The curse will be removed when the serpent and his armies are destroyed; not eliminated, but confined to the everlasting lake of fire never again to interfere in God's plan for His chosen.

Cain was 'of the evil one'

As previously outlined, Abel's offering of the firstborn of his flock was accepted by God while Cain's offering of the fruit of the ground did not gain God's approval. As a result Cain became very angry.

"...And it came about when they were in the field, that Cain rose up against Abel his brother and killed him." Genesis 4:8 NASB

The killing of one's brother was described as 'sin' and was so significant that New Testament writers spoke of it along with describing the two brothers.

"...the one who practices sin is of the devil; for the devil has sinned from the beginning...By this the children of God and the children of the devil are obvious; any one who does not practice righteousness is not of God, nor the one who does not love his brother. For this is the message which you have heard from the beginning, that we should love one

another; not as Cain, who was of the evil one, and slew his brother." 1 John 3:8, 10-12 NASB

John clearly differentiates between those who are children of God and those who are offspring of the wicked one, i.e. the serpent, or devil. And John clearly states that Cain's evil deed identified him with his 'father' the evil one.

Jude, a half-brother of Jesus, also equated deceit and evil with Cain. Speaking of such who had infiltrated the early church:

"But these men revile the things which they do not understand; and the things which they know by instinct, like unreasoning animals. By these things they are destroyed. Woe to them! For they have gone the way of Cain..." Jude 10-11 NASB

Therefore, when a man acts on natural inclinations and dismisses spiritual revelations, he is acting on behalf of his father, the serpent.

Seed of the serpent is represented by tares

Jesus taught many truths relative to His kingdom in parables. When asked by His disciples why He spoke in parables, Jesus responded:

"...to you it has been granted to know the mysteries of the kingdom of heaven, but to them it has not been granted." Matthew 13:11 NASB

He also told them the truths revealed to them were desired by godly men for generations but were reserved for the present age.

"But blessed are your eyes, because they see; and your ears, because they hear. For truly I say to you, that many prophets and righteous men desired to see what you see, and did not see it; and to hear what you hear, and did not hear it." Matthew 13:16-17 NASB

The parables spoken by Jesus revealed mysteries of God's plan that He set forth before time began or the earth was ever prepared for man.

"...I WILL UTTER THINGS HIDDEN SINCE THE FOUNDATION OF THE WORLD." Matthew 13:35 NASB

One of the great parables that speak of the serpent's deceit is the parable of the wheat and tares.

Jesus likened the kingdom of heaven to a man who sowed good seed (wheat) in his field. After he sowed his field an enemy came and spread tares among the good seed. Shortly thereafter the man's servants noted that tares had grown up among the wheat and blamed it on an enemy.

They asked if they should remove the tares from the field but the man told them to let them grow together until the harvest, so as not to damage the wheat while removing the tares. Then at the time of harvest, the tares would be gathered first and be burned up, and then the wheat would be safely harvested.

'Tares' in the Greek means a plant that looks like a wheat stalk when growing, but does not produce any usable fruit. In other words, it is a type of weed that can hardly be distinguished from wheat until it matures.

Then Jesus explained the parable of the tares and wheat to His disciples.

"...The one who sows the good seed is the Son of Man, and the field is the world; and as for the good seed, these are the sons of the kingdom; and the tares are the sons of the evil one; and the enemy who sowed them is the devil, and the harvest is the end of the age; and the reapers are angels. Therefore just as the tares are gathered up and burned with fire, so shall it be at the end of the age." Matthew 13:37-40 NASB

During the present age of the church, or the Kingdom age, it can be expected that many of the enemy's offspring or seeds are occupying places in the church pretending to be what they are not.

Recall evangelist Billy Graham estimated that two out of three church members are not really Christians.

Seeds of the enemy have false security

Perhaps the most contentious group that Jesus dealt with was the Pharisees. A major goal of the Pharisees was to kill Jesus for blasphemy.

The Pharisees denied Jesus' claim of deity and proclaimed their security and favor of God by being offspring of Abraham. Jesus boldly told them that if they were Abraham's children they wouldn't want to kill Him.

Jesus went on to tell them that they were actually seeds of the devil.

"Why do you not understand what I am saying? It is because you cannot hear My word. You are of your father the devil, and you want to do the desires of your father. He was a murderer from the beginning, and does not stand in the truth, because there is no truth in him. Whenever he speaks a lie, he speaks from his own nature; for he is a liar, and the father of lies." John 8:43-44 NASB

Many believe that when Jesus said the devil was a murderer from the beginning, He was referring to Cain murdering his brother Abel. Jesus was actually referring to the Pharisees' 'father' the devil.

The Pharisees hated Jesus even more after that confrontation and sought all the harder to find opportunity to kill Him, but His time had not yet arrived.

Jesus very plainly told the Pharisees that not all sons of Abraham were of God and safe. That great truth was reaffirmed in Paul's writings.

"...For they are not all Israel who are descended from Israel; neither are they all children because they are Abraham's descendants, but: THROUGH ISAAC YOUR DESCENDANTS WILL BE NAMED." Romans 9:6-7 NASB

Recall the frequently listed recipients of God's covenant and blessings in the Old Testament were Abraham, Isaac, and Jacob. The Bible is absolutely clear on the matter.

The truth of Jesus' deity is the major topic of the Apostle John's writings.

A much lengthier discussion on the topic of the sons of Abraham can be found in my previous book entitled *America's Vision vs. God's Standard of Justice.*

Sons of Hades

Jesus also addressed the scribes and Pharisees as sons of Hades because of their hypocrisy. They said but didn't do.

"Woe to you, scribes and Pharisees, hypocrites, because you travel about on sea and land to make one proselyte; and when he becomes one, you make him twice as much a son of (Hades) as yourselves." Matthew 23:15 NASB

Just prior to the above verse in Matthew Jesus said that the Pharisees with their false doctrine were shutting the door to the kingdom of heaven not only for themselves but for others that accepted their teachings.

The Pharisees boasted that if they had lived in the days of their fathers they would not have participated in the shedding of blood of the prophets.

Jesus rebuked their claim and responded that they were sons of those who murdered the prophets beginning with righteous Abel.

He also referred to them as serpents and vipers.

Other seeds of the serpent

In the Book of Acts, Luke records an incident where a sorcerer attempted to thwart the teaching of the word of God.

A proconsul, or Roman government official, wanted to hear Barnabas and Saul (Paul) speak, but the sorcerer Elymas opposed them. He did not want the proconsul to hear the truth. Paul really let him have it.

"But Saul, who was also known as Paul, filled with the Holy Spirit, fixed his gaze upon him, and said, 'You who are full of all deceit and fraud, you son of the devil, you enemy of all righteousness, will you not cease to make crooked the straight ways of the Lord?'" Acts 13:9-10 NASB

Paul continued, "…the hand of the Lord is upon you, and you shall be blind, not seeing the sun for a time" and immediately the man was struck with blindness.

As the proconsul witnessed those events he believed and was 'astonished at the teaching of the Lord.'

Note that Paul under the power of the Holy Spirit rebuked heresy with great boldness and authority - a great lesson for today.

Without a doubt, seeds of the serpent are alive and well, deceiving and enticing all who will give ear. The church needs to be aware and take a firm stand!

"But we should always give thanks to God for you, brethren beloved by the Lord, because God has chosen you from the beginning for salvation through sanctification by the Spirit and faith in the truth…So then, brethren, stand firm and hold to the traditions which you were taught, whether by word of mouth or by letter from us." 2 Thessalonians 2:13, 15 NASB

Chapter 16

Differentiating the
Majority from the Minority

Thus far Scripture has revealed that only a minority, a small part of mankind or a remnant will be redeemed or delivered from God's righteous judgment. There will be a remnant from the nation of Israel and a remnant from all nations, tongues, tribes and peoples from all ages, of which the church is part.

In addition, the earth itself will be redeemed with the removal of the curse pronounced in the third chapter of Genesis.

Then according to the Bible, if only a small part of mankind will place their trust in God and His word, i.e. the minority or remnant, what about the majority?

In other words, what are those who do not take seriously God's word preoccupied with? What are the priorities of those during this present age that have focused on the here and now? What determines their values and actions?

Firstly, differences between the minority and the majority need to be established. In the following, the minority will be referred to as citizens of the kingdom while the majority will be referred to simply as the 'world.'

Defining the 'world'

There are several definitions of 'world,' depending on the context. In the present discussion the focus will be on organized mankind inhabiting the earth without God. The Greek base for this definition is *kosmos*.

The world is concerned with the visible and tangible (material) rather than the invisible and spiritual. It can be considered transience vs. the eternal.

Citizens of the world are indifferent to spiritual truths.

The differences between the world and the kingdom are so profound that there is enmity or hatred between them. Such enmity began ages ago in the garden resulting from the great deception as previously noted.

"And I will put enmity between you and the woman, and between your seed and her Seed..." Genesis 3:15 NKJV

The citizens of the world are not redeemed or regenerated with the new birth, i.e. the majority of mankind does not have the Spirit of God within them. The worldly are governed and motivated by their innate natural instincts.

Godly wisdom vs. worldly wisdom

The Apostle Paul differentiates clearly between the wisdom of God and the wisdom of the world which dominates this current age. This 'age' covers the time span between the establishment of the church and the return of Christ.

"...but God has chosen the foolish things of the world to shame the wise, and God has chosen the weak things of the world to shame the things which are strong, and the base things of the world and the despised, God has chosen, the things that are not, that He might nullify the things that are..." 1 Corinthians 1:27-28 NASB

Paul makes it abundantly clear that the philosophies of the worldly wise, those that depend on their own logic and reasoning, are in direct opposition with the wisdom of God.

"Let no man deceive himself. If any man among you thinks that he is wise in this age, let him become foolish that he may become wise. For the wisdom of this world is foolishness before God..." 1 Corinthians 3:18-19a NASB

The minority remnant is said to be mature, having Godly wisdom vs. wisdom of this age. Rulers of this age who depend on worldly wisdom will come to naught.

"However, we speak wisdom among those who are mature, yet not the wisdom of this age, nor of the rulers

of this age, who are coming to nothing." 1 Corinthians 2:6 NKJV

When Paul addressed the church at Corinth he emphasized that he spoke the wisdom of God and not of his own.

"And my message and my preaching were not in persuasive words of wisdom, but in demonstration of the Spirit and of power, that your faith should not rest on the wisdom of men, but on the power of God." 1 Corinthians 2:4-5 NASB

Therefore, the wisdom of the world and the wisdom of God have absolutely nothing in common.

Godly wisdom (wisdom from above) is embodied in Christ

"...you are in Christ Jesus, who became to us wisdom from God, and righteousness and sanctification, and redemption." 1 Corinthians 1:30 NASB

Christ came into the world to reveal the wisdom of God. He was totally qualified to do this inasmuch as He was God.

The Apostle John wrote extensively about the humanity of Christ as he described Christ's incarnation, His mission, and His rejection by man, even though He was the One who created them.

"He was in the world, and the world was made through Him, and the world did not know Him. He came to His own, and those who were His own did not receive Him." John 1:10-11 NASB

Jesus, the express image of God, came (was born) into the world as the Seed of the woman to reveal truth and divine wisdom. The world did not know Him or receive Him.

During His earthly ministry Christ boldly proclaimed who He was and His purpose.

"...it is My Father who gives you the true bread out of heaven, for the bread of God is that which comes down out of heaven, and gives life to the world...I am the living bread that came down out of heaven; if any one eats of this bread, he shall live forever; and the bread also which I shall give for the life of the world is My flesh." John 6:32-33, 51 NASB

Then Jesus further described Himself as the Light of the world, i.e. enlightenment of the truth.

"Again therefore Jesus spoke to them(scribes and Pharisees) saying 'I am the light of the world; he who follows Me shall not walk in the darkness, but shall have the light of life...you are from below, I am from above; you are of this world; I am not of this world.'" John 8:12, 23 NASB

He confirmed that while He was in the world, He was the light or wisdom of God offered to the world.

"While I am in the world, I am the light of the world."
John 9:5 NASB

"I have come as light into the world, that everyone who believes in Me may not remain in darkness...for I did not come to judge the world, but to save the world." John 12:46-47 NASB

And while Jesus came to earth to redeem the chosen from the world, He will return to judge the world, inasmuch as the majority will have rejected Him and Godly wisdom.

Jesus confirmed to Pilate that the kingdom that He represented was not of the world.

"...My kingdom is not of this world, If My kingdom were of this world, then My servants would be fighting, that I might not be delivered up to the Jews; but as it is, My kingdom is not of this realm." John 18:36 NASB

The world is in direct opposition to the kingdom

The Bible spells out in great detail that kingdom values focus on the invisible and eternal while worldly values focus on the visible and temporary. There is no compromise between the two.

"...while we look not at the things which are seen, but at the things which are not seen; for the things which are seen are temporal, but the things which are not seen are eternal." 2 Corinthians 4:18 NASB

The appearance of Christ and the New Testament presented an entirely different perspective to the world. The focus switched from worldly perceptions of wisdom to the reality of God's spiritual kingdom embodied in Christ. Even the pious had difficulty believing.

Recall Jesus' conversation with Nicodemus:

"If I told you earthly things and you do not believe, how shall you believe if I tell you heavenly things?" John 3:12 NASB

Jesus began to teach His disciples about the reality of the invisible kingdom.

"...that is the Spirit of truth, whom the world cannot receive, because it does not behold Him or know Him, but you know Him because He abides with you, and will be in you." John 14:17 NASB

The world is at total odds with the spiritual kingdom. The world offers rewards here and now while the kingdom offers unseen rewards in the future throughout eternity. The choice is one or the other; there is absolutely no in between or middle of the road.

"No one can serve two masters; for either he will hate the one and love the other, or he will hold to one and despise the other. You cannot serve God and mammon." Matthew 6:24 NASB

'Mammon' in the Greek means 'wealth, riches, possessions, and/or material value.' In essence 'mammon' represents that which is tangible and will subsequently decay and disappear. It means to have plenty in this life and to prosper currently.

Consider Eve's thinking when confronted with the fruit of the tree of the knowledge of good and evil.

"When the woman saw that the tree was good for food, and that it was a delight to the eyes, and that the tree was desirable to make one wise, she took from its fruit and ate..." Genesis 3:5 NASB

Eve was more concerned about satisfying current perceived needs and desires than the consequences of her choice.

The Apostle John stressed that same immutable truth relative to satisfying natural or worldly desires and temptations.

"Do not love the world, nor the things in the world. If any one loves the world, the love of the Father is not in him. For all that is in the world, the lust of the flesh and the lust of the eyes and the boastful pride of life, is not from the Father, but is from the world. And the world is passing away, and also its lusts; but the one who does the will of God abides forever." 1 John 2:15-17 NASB

Jesus summarized the destiny of those who choose the present worldly life instead of unseen eternal life.

"He who loves his life loses it; and he who hates his life in this world shall keep it to life eternal." John 12:25 NASB

But in view of all that, Jesus came into the world with the free offer of redemption to deliver His Father's chosen out of the world.

"For God so loved the world, that He gave His only begotten Son, that whoever believes in Him should not perish, but have eternal life." John 3:16 NASB

The great truth is that everyone born into the world who is not delivered from it will perish.

The worldly majority is concerned with their own

Man makes the choice whether to seek the approval and praise of man or the One who made him. The Pharisees definitely sought the praise of other men rather than the praise of God.

Not much has changed for the contemporary majority.

Jesus differentiated between those who sought glory from other men and those that sought glory and approval from God.

The men-pleasers are more concerned with 'I' vs. 'He.'

Recall the parable of the Pharisee and the tax collector.

"The Pharisee stood and was praying thus to himself, 'God, I thank Thee that I am not like other people: swindlers, unjust, adulterers, or even like this tax-gatherer. I fast twice a week; I pay tithes of all that I get...'" Luke 8:11-12 NASB

Jesus went on to explain that the one who exalts himself before men and God will be humbled, and the one that humbles himself before men and God will be exalted.

Man-pleasing was a common topic in Jesus' teachings.

"He who speaks from himself seeks his own glory; but He who is seeking the glory of the one who sent Him, He is true, and there is no unrighteousness in Him." John 7:18 NASB

The Greek for 'glory' has several significant synonyms including 'praise' and 'honor.' When men seek glory for themselves it typically relates to the favorable opinion of other men.

Jesus was explaining that He sought only the glory of His Father.

"I do not receive glory from men; but I know you, that you do not have the love of God in yourselves. I have come in My Father's name, and you do not receive Me...How can you believe, when you receive glory from one another,

and you do not seek the glory that is from the one and only God?" John 5:41-44 NASB

Jesus continued by explaining that the love of God was not in a man who sought honor and glory from other men rather than seeking the honor that comes from the one and only God.

And while many believed in Jesus and His message, they kept silent so as to please the crowd.

"Nevertheless many even of the rulers believed in Him, but because of the Pharisees they were not confessing Him... for they loved the approval (praise) of men rather than the approval of God." John 12:42-43 NASB

Even the powerful Roman Governor Pontius Pilate succumbed to the demands of the Jewish leaders.

"And wishing to satisfy the multitude, Pilate released Barabbas for them..." Mark 15:15 NASB

And today, as it was two thousand years ago, the majority on the wide road is more concerned with peer approval than they are with seeking God's approval, regardless of the truth.

The effort today to avoid offending others has really put America on a slippery slope. A major aspect is appeasing those who are offended by Christianity either in spoken word, deed, or display.

'Civil rights' are taking precedence over Christian values.

Polls and probability

Polls and probability are closely related and are based on the mathematical likelihood, or percentage, of a future event becoming reality.

Many politicians of today claim they don't follow the polls, especially if such polls are not favorable to them. Others say the polls are a good indicator of the future, if such polls reflect them in a favorable light.

But in God's sovereignty, how significant are polls?

Beginning in the early days of Israel, apportionments and appointments were made, not by polls and probability, but by casting lots.

"These are the areas which the children of Israel inherited in the land of Canaan...Their inheritance was by lot, as the LORD had commanded by the hand of Moses..." Joshua 14:1-2 NKJV

Such was the method also used to select individuals.

"And they said to one another, 'Come, let us cast lots, that we may know for whose cause this trouble has come upon us.' So they cast lots, and the lot fell on Jonah." Jonah 1:7 NKJV

Now before we conclude that there was 'chance' involved, we need to see how Solomon explained the casting of lots.

"The lot is cast...but its every decision is from the LORD." Proverbs 16:33 NKJV

The Hebrew for 'lot' means 'destiny.' The Hebrew for 'decision' has several interesting synonyms including 'judgment, justice, right,' and/or 'law.'

Therefore, according to God's predetermined sovereign choice, the lot fell accordingly in every instance.

Let's jump forward to the New Testament. The event was choosing a replacement disciple for Judas.

"And they proposed two: Joseph called Barsabas...and Matthias. And they prayed and said, 'You, O Lord, who know the hearts of all, show which of these two You have chosen to take part in this ministry and apostleship from which Judas by transgression fell...' And they cast their lots, and the lot fell on Matthias." Acts 1:23-26 NKJV

But God's choice of the individuals to participate in His plan is far more encompassing than illustrated by the casting of lots. His complete sovereignty was made known from the beginning.

For example, hundreds of years before Israel demanded a king, God had revealed they would indeed have a king; a king that God Himself would choose.

"When you come to the land which the LORD your God is giving you...and say, 'I will set a king over me like all the nations that are around me,' you shall surely set a king over you whom the LORD your God chooses; one from among your brethren...you may not set a foreigner over you, who is not your brother." Deuteronomy 17:15-16 NKJV

High points from the above include God's proclamation that He would choose Israel's king and the king would be an Israelite, i.e. one who shared the ideology and religion given to national Israel.

Further in that passage God said that the future king would study the same law given to the priests all the days of his life to insure understanding and compliance with God's required standard of justice.

Approximately 800 years later God reiterated His sovereignty in choosing kings and kingdoms.

"...the Most High rules in the kingdom of men, gives it to whomever He will, and sets over it the lowest of men." Daniel 4:17b NKJV

This verse applied to the Babylonian king Nebuchadnezzar. However, the same principle applied when God gave Israel king Saul to teach them a lesson. He gave them what they wanted and deserved. Sound familiar?

Well nothing has changed. God is still very active in American politics and the choosing of our leaders.

"Let every soul be subject to the governing authorities. For there is no authority except from God, and the authorities that exist are appointed by God." Romans 13:1 NKJV

The sovereignty of God in the affairs of mankind is beyond finite man's ability to comprehend.

The recognition of God's sovereignty does not negate the Christian's responsibility to support the candidate who best represents God's standard of righteousness, while being willing to accept God's choice, for He does nothing without reason.

What do you suppose the 'chances' are that one of the presidential candidates will adopt the following motto in question form, i.e. "Are we closer to God's standard of righteousness today than 8 years ago?"

Who should we fear and trust?

One of the most basic questions that have faced all mankind through the ages, and particularly America today is who or what is worthy of trust?

And once again as would be expected, the choice boils down to whether trust is better placed in the created or the Creator; in the seen or the unseen; the world or the kingdom; the majority or the minority.

The Scriptures speak loudly of the choice and the reasoning for the choice.

"...Who are you that you are afraid of man who dies, and of the son of man who is made like grass; that you have forgotten the LORD your Maker, who stretched out the heavens, and laid the foundations of the earth..." Isaiah 51:12-13 NASB

God inquires of Israel why they would place their trust and confidence in 'man' who is transitory and not in the One that created him.

The Hebrew for 'afraid' means 'fearful anticipation of potential harm.' And the Hebrew for 'forgotten' means 'to be oblivious to for lack of attention,' i.e. it is a conscious setting aside of something known or proven.

To forget is so much more than a slip of the mind; it is a deliberate action.

The wisest man in the world, Solomon, also addressed the issue.

"The fear of man brings a snare, but he who trusts in the LORD will be exalted. Many seek the ruler's favor but justice for man comes from the LORD." Proverbs 29:25-26 NASB

The fear of what transitory man could do is really a snare, i.e. trap, but can be avoided by trusting in the One who made man.

Solomon reminded the people that justice for man does not rest with the ruler or king but rather with God Himself.

Misplaced trust is not new

The prophet Jeremiah clearly delineated the two choices, i.e. to either trust in man or the LORD.

"...Cursed is the man who trusts in mankind and makes flesh his strength, and whose heart turns away from the LORD. For he will be like a bush in the desert...Blessed is the man who trusts in the LORD and whose trust is the LORD. For he will be like a tree planted by the water..." Jeremiah 17:5-6a, 7-8a NASB

Therefore, when congressional leaders draft legislation or the president prepares an executive order, is God's word consulted for adherence to His standard of righteousness and justice or is reliance and trust placed on polling data?

Coalition building

During the past several decades the United States has not confronted an enemy nation without first obtaining a consensus from other nations. The reasons are twofold, i.e.

to convince ourselves that we are doing the right thing and to increase our perceived power against the enemy.

The reliance on other nations instead of God was a major problem with the Israelites throughout their history. God told them in no uncertain terms such strategy was totally foolish.

"Woe to the rebellious children...who execute a plan, but not Mine, and make an alliance, but not of My Spirit... who proceed down to Egypt, without consulting Me, to take refuge in the safety of Pharaoh, and to seek shelter in the shadow of Egypt!" Isaiah 30:1-2 NASB

The simple message was that it was utterly foolish for a nation to look to other nations and men for advice and counsel instead of invoking the One who created man and divided the nations.

God then mocked Israel for trusting in the military strength of Egypt, or any other nation, especially an enemy nation.

"Woe to those who go down to Egypt for help, and rely on horses, and trust in chariots because they are many, and in horsemen because they are very strong, but they do not look to the Holy One of Israel, nor seek the LORD! ...Now the Egyptians are men, and not God, and their horses are flesh and not spirit; so the LORD will stretch out His hand, and he who helps will stumble and he who is helped will

fall, and all of them will come to an end together." Isaiah 31:1, 3 NASB

Is there a time in recent history when America turned to God for counsel for protection against an enemy nation instead of relying on a multinational coalition?

The Bible describes the world as corrupt and depraved

Peter confirmed that citizens of the kingdom would be delivered from the corrupt world.

"...you might become partakers of the divine nature, having escaped the corruption (depravity) that is in the world by lust." 2 Peter 1:4b NASB

God's offer of redemption included the fact that partakers of the kingdom would be conformed to the image of His Son.

Likewise Paul warned not to be conformed to the world.

"And do not be conformed to this world, but be transformed by the renewing of your mind, that you may prove what the will of God is, that which is good and acceptable and perfect." Romans 12:2 NASB

Again, being conformed to the world is directly opposite to being conformed to the image of Christ.

Those being conformed to the image of Christ are in turn called to enlighten those of the world in the current generation.

"...that you may prove yourselves to be blameless and innocent, children of God above reproach in the midst of a crooked and perverse generation, among whom you appear as lights in the world." Philippians 2:15 NASB

Animosity between the world and the kingdom

The world was delighted that Jesus would be killed and be gone while the redeemed would be saddened.

"Truly, truly, I say to you, that you will weep and lament, but the world will rejoice; you will be sorrowful, but your sorrow will be turned to joy." John 16:20 NASB

The animosity became hatred. The world would not only hate the Redeemer, but also the redeemed. And so it is today.

"If the world hates you, you know that it has hated Me before it hated you. If you were of the world, the world would love its own; but because you are not of the world, but I chose you out of the world, therefore the world hates you." John 15:18-19 NASB

During Jesus intercessory prayer for His disciples He reiterated the world's hatred for His own.

"I have given them Thy word; and the world has hated them, because they are not of the world, even as I am not of the world...As Thou didst send Me into the world, I also have sent them into the world." John 17:14-18 NASB

And later in his epistles John confirmed the enmity between the world and the kingdom.

"See how great a love the Father has bestowed upon us, that we should be called children of God; and such we are. For this reason the world does not know us, because it did not know Him...Do not marvel, brethren, if the world hates you." 1 John 3:1, 13 NASB

James had a similar message to professing Christians (hypocrites) but didn't possess saving faith. Such were committing spiritual adultery.

"You adulteresses, do you not know that friendship with the world is hostility toward God? Therefore whoever wishes to be a friend of the world makes himself an enemy of God." James 4:4 NASB

The ruler of the world

The ruler of the world who is in direct opposition to God is of course the devil himself. The devil has no power over the Redeemer and will end up in the lake of fire. Jesus said:

"...for the ruler of this world is coming, and he has nothing in Me." John 14:30 NASB

The Apostle John summarized Jesus' purpose very succinctly.

"The Son of God appeared for this purpose, that He might destroy the works of the devil." 1 John 3:8b NASB

Satan's deception began with Eve in the garden and continues to this day.

"We know that we are of God, and the whole world lies in the power of the evil one." 1 John 5:19 NASB

Paul summarily differentiated between the members of the kingdom and those of the world. He stated that all mankind was born into the world, but Christ redeemed the chosen remnant out of the world and made them citizens of the kingdom of heaven.

"...in which you formerly walked according to the course of this world, according to the prince of the power of the air, of the spirit that is now working in the sons of disobedience. Among them we too all formerly lived in the lusts of our flesh and of the mind and were by nature children of wrath..." Ephesians 2:2-3 NASB

The children of the kingdom must not underestimate the nature of the enemy.

"For our struggle is not against flesh and blood, but against the rulers, against the powers, against the world

forces of this darkness, against the spiritual forces of wickedness in the heavenly places." Ephesians 6:12 NASB

Payday will come someday. Jesus said:

"Now judgment is upon this world; now the ruler of this world shall be cast out." John 12:31 NASB

How about today?

The stage has been set. The redeemed minority has been defined as well as the worldly majority. The leader of the kingdom of God has been identified as Christ and the leader of the world has been identified as Satan.

Now the philosophy and ideology of the present day can be examined to see which leader is being followed.

Simply stated, is America as a nation more closely allied with the tenets of the world and its leader or the kingdom and its leader?

Or does America even recognize the difference between the two?

Chapter 17

What in the 'World' is the Majority up to these days?

The Bible states that all nations are involved in harlotry, i.e. spiritual adultery. Does that mean that America has also lowered herself to such depravity?

Several Biblical passages can be examined to answer that question. Let's begin with a passage penned nearly 3,500 years ago.

"Beware lest you forget the LORD your God by not keeping His commandments and His ordinances and His statutes which I am commanding you today; lest, when you have eaten and are satisfied, and have built good houses and lived in them, and when your herds and your flocks multiply, and your silver and gold multiply, and all that you have multiplies, then your heart becomes proud, and you forget the LORD your God..." Deuteronomy 8:11-14 NASB

The major point is that God would provide Israel all she could ever dream of having. When the promises came to fruition in their new land, they were not to forget the source of their prosperity and blessings.

They were not to boast nor take credit for anything God had provided.

"Otherwise, you may say in your heart, 'My power and the strength of my hand made me this wealth.'" Deuteronomy 8:17 NASB

Approximately 800 years later, after a history of disobedience, God recounted Israel's required judgment. Both northern Israel and southern Judah were labeled as harlots because they had committed spiritual adultery against their betrothed.

"Therefore, thus says the Lord GOD, 'Because you have forgotten Me and cast Me behind your back, bear now the punishment (penalty) of your lewdness and your harlotries.'" Ezekiel 23:35 NASB

Recall the Hebrew for 'forgotten' means 'to be oblivious to because of lack of attention,' i.e. a conscious forsaking.

The word 'lewdness' means 'evil' or 'wicked,' while 'cast' means 'to consciously put someone or something away.'

The phrase 'bear the punishment' means 'to accept, receive, or carry the penalty.'

And the word 'harlotry' means metaphorically 'idolatry' in addition to 'spiritual adultery.' Depending on the context it can also mean 'illegal contact between Israel and other nations.' For Israel to depend on other nations or coalitions for their safety instead of God was considered to be harlotry.

Harlotry is mentioned throughout the Bible and is summarized in the Book of Revelation where the great harlot is called the mother of harlots.

"...she glorified herself and lived sensuously (luxuriously)...for she says in her heart, 'I sit as a queen and I am not a widow, and will never see mourning (sorrow)...'" Revelation 18:7 NASB

The great harlot epitomizes the world and temporal abundance

The Bible reveals that the final ten nation confederation (coalition) under the ruler of the seventh and final world kingdom will destroy her.

"And the ten horns which you saw, and the beast, these will hate the harlot and will make her desolate and naked, and will eat her flesh and will burn her up with fire." Revelation 17:16 NASB

Who will miss her the most?

"And the merchants of the earth will weep and mourn over her, for no one buys their merchandise anymore." Revelation 18:11 NKJV

Several questions arise:

Has America also forsaken her God and committed adultery by placing her faith and trust in capitalism and materialism? Are trade and material things more important to America than her relationship with God?

Is America more concerned with transitory things than eternal things? Has America's value system been transformed to focus on the here and now?

If the answers to the above questions are 'yes,' then America has been deceived and been led down the path to harlotry. However, she is not alone.

"For all the nations have drunk of the wine of the wrath of her fornication, the kings of the earth have committed fornication with her, and the merchants of the earth have become rich through the abundance of her luxury." Revelation 18:3 NKJV

The second word in the above passage is 'all.'

There is much comfort in knowing that a person is not 'saved' based on the performance of the nation in which he/she lives. A person is saved with a one-on-one relationship with the Lamb of God. The congregate of such in the present age is called the 'church.'

And while many individual people will repent, no nation other than Israel is promised eternal existence as a nation.

Several contemporary issues that reflect America's progressivism

In the summer of 2015 the Supreme Court ruled to legalize same-sex marriage in every state. On one side of the issue is President Obama's progressive view and on the other side is the Biblical view.

The Biblical view is clearly outlined in several passages.

In President Obama's victory speech following the Supreme Court's decision, he repeatedly stressed the importance of equality as justification for his approval of the court's decision.

"This morning, the Supreme Court...reaffirmed that all Americans are entitled to the equal protection of the law..."

"And this ruling is a victory for America. This decision affirms what millions of Americans already believe in their hearts. When all Americans are treated as equal, we are all more free."

"I know that Americans of good will continue to hold a wide range of views on this issue. Opposition, in some cases, has been based on sincere and deeply held beliefs."

The president's advice to minimize the conflict:

"But today should also give us hope that on the many issues with which we grapple, often painfully, real change is possible. Shift in hearts and minds is possible."

The president stated that those who cling to Biblical teachings should reexamine their thinking and be willing to compromise.

In his concluding remarks he said with 'certainty' that the farther America strays from Biblical principles the 'more perfect' she becomes.

"But today, we can say in no uncertain terms that we've made our union a little more perfect."

His summary statement:

"America should be very proud."

Demonic activity in the 'here and now'

Many are unwilling to accept that demonic activity permeates the political process in America today.

Demons are spirits of fallen angels. While many demons are temporarily confined to the bottomless pit, many are very active in world affairs today serving their master the

Devil. In fact demons are perhaps the major implementers of Satan's deceitful agenda.

And many of those imprisoned demons in the bottomless pit will be released during the rapidly approaching tribulation period to punish unrepentant mankind. We'll examine that aspect shortly.

Demonic activity isn't new. Such activity was noted in ancient Israel as well as spoken of in the New Testament including the final book of the Bible, i.e. the Revelation of Jesus Christ.

Let's go back several thousand years and review a profound passage from the Psalms that describes the range of Israel's sins.

"They served their (Gentile's) idols...They even sacrificed their sons and their daughters to demons, and shed innocent blood, the blood of their sons and daughters..." Psalm 106:36-38a NKJV

But the influence of demons goes far beyond sacrifices; it includes false and deceitful teaching.

"Now the Spirit expressly (explicitly) says that in latter times some will depart from the faith, giving heed to deceiving spirits and doctrines of demons, speaking lies in hypocrisy..." 1 Timothy 4:1-2a NKJV

Anyone who 'will depart from the faith' is called an 'apostate.' Paul warned that there would be great apostasy before Christ returns.

Submission to demonic influence will accelerate during this age and come to a head during the great tribulation. Regardless of the extent of tribulation hardship, the nonbeliever will cling to demonically inspired idols.

The sixth trumpet judgment during the great tribulation describes the refusal of nonbelievers to repudiate demonic influence.

Demons from the bottomless pit will be released to kill one-third of mankind and yet those who survive will not repent from demon worship.

"But the rest of mankind, who were not killed by these plagues, did not repent of the works of their hands, that they should not worship demons, and idols of gold, silver, brass, stone, and wood, which can neither see nor hear nor walk." Revelation 9:20 NKJV

Non-repentant mankind will continue to place their trust in idols of gold, silver, etc.

Then John lists several other activities that nonbelievers will not abandon.

"And they did not repent of their murders or their sorceries or their sexual immorality or their thefts." Revelation 9:21 NKJV

Murder *(phonos)* means 'slaughter, butcher, cut to pieces.'

Sorcery *(pharmakeia)* means 'drugs, occult, or magical incantation with drugs.'

Sexual immorality *(porneia)* includes any kind of sexual sin.

Thefts *(klepto)* means not only 'to steal,' but has additional synonyms including 'seize, or take by deceit.'

Using the four preceding definitions, does killing the unborn by cutting them to pieces and selling their body parts fit the description of murder?

Does the legalization of marijuana fit the description of sorcery?

Does the mandate by the Supreme Court to recognize the marriage between two people of the same gender fit the description of sexual immorality?

Does the redistribution of wealth by way of taxation to fund activities performed by Planned Parenthood fit the description of thievery?

If any of the above practices or activities are not initiated or sanctioned by God, where does the thoughts for such legislation, Supreme Court decisions, or executive orders originate?

"Who is wise and understanding among you? Let him show by good conduct that his works are done in the meekness of wisdom. But if you have bitter envy and self-seeking in your hearts, do not boast...This wisdom does not descend from above, but is earthly, sensual, demonic." James 3:13-15 NKJV

The folly of expending effort on that which man cannot control

One of the follies of the world is trying to usurp God's sovereign power by attempting to change things over which man has no control.

For example, climate change is being given top priority by many world leaders today even though proof that mankind has any control over climate change or weather patterns is lacking.

As would be expected, the Bible addresses both weather patterns and climate change along with their causes.

"But it shall come to pass, if you do not obey the voice of the LORD your God, to observe carefully all His commandments...the LORD will send on you cursing,

*confusion, and rebuke in all that you set your hand to do...
the LORD will change the rain of your land to powder and
dust..."* Deuteronomy 28:15, 20, 24 NKJV

Inasmuch as God created the rain, He also controls it
at His will and may withhold it as a disciplinary action
for disobedience. The above instructions were given to
the Israelites just prior to entering the Promised Land of
Canaan.

God has power over extreme climate changes just as He
has power over variable weather patterns.

*"Then the fourth angel poured out his bowl on the sun,
and power was given to him to scorch men with fire. And
men were scorched with great heat, and they blasphemed
the name of God who has power over these plagues (from
the Greek plege, i.e. calamities); and they did not repent
and give Him glory."* Revelation 16:8-9 NKJV

President Obama has addressed the issue of climate
change numerous times and in various places. The following
is taken from his 2014 State of the Union Address.

"But the debate is settled. Climate change is a fact.
And when our children's children look us in the eye and
ask if we did all we could to leave them a safer, more
stable world...I want us to be able to say yes, we did."

Several months later while addressing the UN, President
Obama reiterated his conviction that climate change was

the biggest threat to the world. His address was one day after the initial bombing attack in Syria.

"Climate change is the most consequential, urgent, sweeping collection of challenges we face as a nation and a world."

Interestingly just several weeks prior to the president's UN address, Secretary of State Kerry and former Secretary Clinton delivered the same message. Their messages also involved political correctness, i.e. Kerry addressed a Muslim audience stating that 'our faiths are inextricably linked on the environment.' Secretary Clinton addressed the National Clean Air Summit.

Then more recently on October 14, 2015 Obama doubled down on his naiveté while addressing graduates at the Coast Guard Academy.

"I am here today to say that climate change constitutes a serious threat to global security, an immediate risk to our national security, and, make no mistake, it will impact how our military defends our country...Climate change, and especially rising seas, is a threat to our homeland security, our economic infrastructure, the safety and health of the American..."

The greatest difference between God's control of the rain and drought in the Old Testament is that He initially gave Israel a choice to repent and obey which would result in life giving rain.

The catastrophic climate changes described in the Book of Revelation can be classified as pre-written history. There is no opportunity for man to repent now or in the future that could prevent those judgments.

Foreign policy without God overstates man's power

The following sections will reflect the ideology of President Obama. Inasmuch as he was elected for two terms by majority vote, he must have reflected the mindset of the majority of citizens.

The presidency of the United States is considered by the majority to be the most powerful position in the 'free world.'

In September 2014 Thomas Friedman wrote an op-ed column for the New York Times entitled: ***Obama on the World.***

The column title was perfectly appropriate inasmuch as President Obama spoke exclusively from a worldly viewpoint. As such his assessment of contemporary foreign policy challenges contained no Kingdom wisdom.

Several words or phrases dominated the president's discourse which characterizes his mindset. He used the word 'compromise' five times in the interview; the word 'maximalist' four times; the phrase 'no victor/no vanquished' three times; and the personal pronoun 'I' more times than the others combined.

One word not used by the president in the interview was 'God.' Either he doesn't believe that God is involved in foreign policy issues, or he chooses to ignore God's participation in, or sovereignty over, such issues.

The major players/issues discussed focused on Middle Eastern nations and the Israeli/Palestinian conflict.

President Obama's overriding philosophy relative to foreign policy is that everyone should be able to co-exist and simply get along peacefully.

He believes that all parties should compromise. The word 'compromise' can be defined as 'to settle by mutual concession.'

The president used the term 'maximalist' in a negative sense as 'one who holds extreme political views and is not willing to compromise.'

As stated, the president injected the phrase 'no victor/ no vanquished' several times. 'Vanquished' means 'to be overcome in battle where there is an obvious victor.' It further means 'to be conquered;' 'to be defeated;' 'to be subdued;' for one 'to gain mastery over another.'

And while the president believes in no victor/no vanquished, the Bible repeatedly tells of the opposite, especially as relates to His chosen nation Israel. Consider the following example where King David extolled God as the victor.

"Blessed are You, LORD God of Israel...Yours, O LORD, is the greatness, the power and the glory, the victory and the majesty; for all that is in heaven and in earth is Yours; Yours is the kingdom, O LORD, and You are exalted as head over all." 1 Chronicles 29:10-11 NKJV

Some might surmise that since David wrote a millennium before Christ was born, God's sovereignty over the nations is no longer relevant.

Consider the Apostle Paul addressing Grecian philosophers during the early days of the church.

"And He has made from one blood every nation of men to dwell on all the face of the earth, and has determined their pre-appointed (appointed) times and the boundaries of their dwellings." Acts 17:26 NKJV

The Greek for 'nation' in the present context means 'the whole race of mankind.'

The Greek for 'determine' means to 'mark out definitely.' Synonyms include 'setting off by boundary,' and/or 'apportioning.'

'Appointed' means 'to cause to do or be' while boundaries means 'a setting of bounds or a limit.'

Is compromise a kingdom premise or a strategy of the world?

President Obama believes that compromise is the key ingredient to achieving peace in the Middle Peace. As mentioned he used the word five times in his recent interview with the New York Times.

During that interview he offered compromise not only as a global solution but also as the near term solution to the chaos in Iraq. The president said:

"But for a society to function long term, the people themselves have to make decisions about how they are going to live together... how they are going to compromise."

Once again, the Scriptures address the issue of compromise. For example after God promised the land of Canaan to the fledgling nation of Israel, did He instruct Joshua to negotiate with the land's inhabitants? Do men determine national boundaries or does God? Moses spoke very succinctly on the issue.

"Give ear, O heavens, and I will speak; and hear, O earth, the words of my mouth...When the Most High divided their inheritance to the nations, when He separated the sons of Adam, He set the boundaries of the peoples according to the number of the children of Israel." Deuteronomy 32:1, 8 NKJV

Moses was addressing the inhabitants of the entire earth and by using the word 'when' he proclaimed that God had already determined the boundaries of all nations. The Apostle Paul reaffirmed Moses' declaration that God had pre-set the boundaries of the nations. Nothing has changed, except that man has steadily distanced himself from God's words.

No compromise with Israel's land

Joshua's taking possession of the land of Canaan is explained in two stages, i.e. the southern conquest and the northern conquest. Concerning the southern conquest of Canaan:

"So Joshua conquered all the land; the mountain country and the South...and all their kings; he left none remaining but utterly destroyed all that breathed, as the LORD God of Israel had commanded." Joshua 10:40 NKJV

No negotiations. Joshua conquered all the land of southern Canaan and destroyed all the kings whom he had displaced; all according to God's instructions.

Then the conquest of the northern part of Canaan is described in great detail. When the kings of the northern portion of Canaan heard of the conquest of the south they joined together to fight Israel.

"And they came out, they and all their armies with them, as many people as the sand that is on the seashore, with very many horses and chariots...to fight against Israel." Joshua 11:4-5 NASB

But God reassured Joshua that the defeat of those kings was certain.

"Then the LORD said to Joshua, 'Do not be afraid because of them, for tomorrow at this time I will deliver all of them slain before Israel...'" Joshua 11:6 NASB

"So all the cites of those kings, and all their kings, Joshua took with the edge of the sword...and all the spoil of these cities and the livestock, the children of Israel took as booty...he (Joshua) left nothing undone of all that the LORD had commanded Moses." Joshua 11:12, 14-15 NKJV

Near the end of the Book of Joshua, the taking of the land is summarized.

"So the LORD gave to Israel all the land of which He had sworn to give to their fathers, and they took possession of it and dwelt in it... the LORD delivered all their enemies into their hand." Joshua 21:43-44 NKJV

Take God at His word

Perhaps the following verse puts Israel's conquests in proper perspective. It should be the benchmark for today's foreign policy decisions and actions.

"Not a word failed of any good thing which the LORD had spoken to the house of Israel. All came to pass." Joshua 21:45 NKJV

President Obama's Bible clearly outlines God's plan for the future. He names those nations to be involved and the future of Israel.

The question is, then; does the president use his Bible as the guide to dealing with the present problems in Iraq? His words describe his solution.

"You're going to have to show us that you are willing and ready to try and maintain a unified Iraqi government that is based on compromise."

Remember, Iraq is the ancient land of Shinar which includes the land between the Tigris and Euphrates Rivers.

President Obama's 'take' on Israel

President Obama was asked recently if he was worried about Israel. The president's response:

"It is amazing to see what Israel has become over the last several decades. To have scratched out of rock this incredibly vibrant, incredibly successful, wealthy and powerful country is a testament to the ingenuity, energy and vision of the Jewish people."

If President Obama's perception of foreign policy relative to Israel is based only on the 'last several decades' he is totally ignoring the big picture.

Israel's past and future history has already been written. There is no room for compromising God's plan based on 'logic' or political correctness. God's preordained odyssey for Israel began 4,000 years ago and is immutable.

It began with a man who lived on the other side of the Euphrates River in a land presently known as Iraq. He was told to leave the gods of that land and travel to a new land which God would show him. Recall that famous calling:

"Get out of your country...I will make you a great nation...and in you all the families of the earth shall be blessed." Genesis 12:2-3 NKJV

Synonyms for the Hebrew word 'families' include 'tribes, race, and people.' In other words, when God scattered the nations after their attempt to build Babel, He declared that peoples from every race and tribe would be blessed through the man called from ancient Iraq, i.e. Abraham.

And then recall God defined the boundaries of the land He would give Abraham for the new nation.

"...To your descendants I have given this land, from the river of Egypt as far as the great river, the river Euphrates..." Genesis 15:18 NASB

Inhabitants of the land, who would subsequently be removed, included the Canaanites who were offspring of Ham who was a son of Noah.

God would bless Israel by making them His chosen nation. He would reveal to this new nation His standard of righteousness and justice. They were to learn His commandments and teach them to all generations.

He then told them some of His provisions.

"So it shall be, when the LORD your God brings you into the land of which He swore to your fathers, to Abraham, Isaac, and Jacob, to give you large and beautiful cities which you did not build, houses full of all good things, which you did not fill, hewn-out wells which you did not dig, vineyards and olive trees which you did not plant – when you have eaten and are full – then beware, lest you forget the LORD who brought you out of the land of Egypt, from the house of bondage." Deuteronomy 6:10-12 NKJV

Therefore, Israel did not 'scratch out of rock' what they have, and their wealth and riches did not begin 'over the last several decades.'

Nothing has changed

God's promise for Israel's blessings through Abraham and his descendants is absolutely immutable and everlasting.

God would provide to His chosen people all that they could ever need, and much more.

God warned the Israelites not to forget his commandments and judgments, i.e. not to willfully neglect them, or they would experience grave consequences. Israel has disobeyed God's commandments throughout their entire history; however, God's covenant with Abraham is forever and will be totally fulfilled upon the return of their Messiah, i.e. the Seed of the woman through Abraham, Isaac, and Jacob... David...

In other words Israel is on a pre-written journey foreordained for them by their God. Any attempt to change or rewrite God's plan for Israel is more than foolish.

Our president's assessment of Israel's present success, or his vision for Israel's future, is naïve at best, or an attempt to play God at worst. His 'take' is totally void of Kingdom wisdom.

America's best foreign policy regarding Israel would be to align our efforts with God's existing, immutable plan for them.

Israel and the Palestinian challenge

President Obama has offered his advice on how best for Israel to preserve their survival.

"...it has consistently been my belief that you have to find a way to live side by side in peace with Palestinians... You have to recognize that they have legitimate claims, and this is their land and neighborhood as well."

Then on October 16, 2015 the president was more specific.

"Over time, the only way that Israel is going to be truly secure, and the only way the Palestinians are going to be able to meet the aspirations of their people, is if they are two states living side by side in peace and security."

President Obama's foreign policy vision is not only naïve, it is totally irrelevant. Concerning Israel's Prime Minister:

"With Prime Minister Netanyahu's poll numbers being so high, it will be hard for him to make some very difficult compromises..."

The very thought of poll numbers being a determining factor in pre-written foreign policy is beyond laughable.

And then closing out the discussion, President Obama offered a challenge to both Israel and the Palestinians.

"It's going to require leadership among both the Palestinians and the Israelis to look beyond tomorrow... And that's the hardest thing for politicians to do is to take the long view on things."

The Bible, however, does offer 'the long view of things' relative to Israel and her neighbors.

The Prophet Isaiah offered details about Israel's relation with the nations surrounding them during the Kingdom following the great tribulation.

"Arise, shine; for your light has come! And the glory of the LORD is risen upon you...The Gentiles shall come to your light, and kings to the brightness of your rising...Lift up your eyes all around, and see: They all gather together, they come to you...The wealth of the Gentiles shall come to you. The multitude of camels shall cover your land..." Isaiah 60:1, 3-4a, 5b-6a NKJV

Therefore, Mr. President, even though you think 'the hardest thing for politicians to do is to take the long view on things,' the long view has already been provided for you. Poll numbers or political correctness needn't even be consulted or considered. Compromise is not an option.

Isaiah then records the fate of the nations who choose not to honor Israel and her future King.

"For the nation and the kingdom which will not serve you will perish, and the nations will be utterly ruined." Isaiah 60:12 NASB

The Bible couldn't be much clearer; it provides succinct prophecy relative to Israel's future as well as the future of those nations (including America) who will not submit to Israel.

Recall that Israel wanted a king so they could be 'like all the nations that are around.'

Instructions for their king included:

"And it shall be with him, and he shall read it (God's law) all the days of his life, that he may learn to fear the LORD his God and be careful to observe all the words of this law...that his heart may not be lifted above his brethren, that he may not turn aside from the commandment to the right hand or to the left..." Deuteronomy 17:19-20 NKJV

That is still good and relevant advice.

President Obama's 'take' on America's strength

On September 10, 2014 President Obama made a prime time speech on foreign policy.

Several relevant statements from his speech include:

"America is better positioned today to seize the future than any other nation on earth."

"...American leadership is the one constant in an uncertain world."

"That is the difference we make in the world."

The sovereignty of God or even the mention of His name did not appear in the speech until the final words.

"...and may God bless the United States of America."

Biblical warning to all nations

Abraham's offspring was the first family to be called a nation. Accordingly, Israel was/is God's chosen and favored nation. And even though Israel is the Apple of God's Eye, they are about to experience severe judgment because of their disobedience.

What about the other nations? What part, if any, do the other nations play in the future history of the earth?

The prophet Isaiah calls all nations to listen as God reveals that all nations have violated His statutes and will taste of His fury.

"Come near, you nations, to hear; and heed, you people! Let the earth hear, and all that is in it...For the indignation of the LORD is against all nations, and His fury against all their armies..." Isaiah 34:1-2 NKJV

Therefore, according to the Bible, all nations will be punished along with God's chosen nation of Israel.

"But the LORD is the true God; He is the living God and the everlasting King. At His wrath the earth will tremble,

and the nations will not be able to endure His indignation."
Jeremiah 10:10 NKJV

The Hebrew for 'wrath' in the above passage means 'fury,' 'indignation,' and/or 'anger.'

Again, according to the Bible, God's wrath will affect all nations 'and the nations will not be able to endure His indignation (wrath).'

Jesus Christ will inflict the Father's wrath on the earth

Progressing to the New Testament, the apostle John reveals that God the Father has delegated all judgment to Jesus, His Son.

"But the Father judges no one, but has committed all judgment to the Son, that all should honor the Son just as they honor the Father. He who does not honor the Son does not honor the Father who sent Him." John 5:22-23 NKJV

At the exact predetermined time in history, Jesus Christ the righteous Judge will return to earth and reestablish God's immutable priorities.

"Now I saw heaven opened, and behold, a white horse. And He who sat on him was called Faithful and True, and in righteousness He judges and makes war." Revelation 19:11 NKJV

The war spoken of will end the great tribulation at which time Christ will reestablish His kingdom in Israel's capital city of Jerusalem. The war will be the greatest war of all time.

"Now out of His mouth goes a sharp sword that with it He should strike the nations. And He Himself will rule them with a rod of iron. He Himself treads the winepress of the fierceness and wrath of Almighty God." Revelation 19:15 NKJV

Therefore, there are several questions all Americans should be asking themselves.

- Is America included when the Bible speaks of 'all' nations?
- Would America ever put the economy or commercialism ahead of God?
- Do America's leaders really take the Bible seriously, or…

"These people draw near to Me with their mouth, and honor Me with their lips, but their heart is far from Me." Matthew 15:8 NKJV

Has America passed the point of no return?

Everyone can draw their own conclusion as to where America stands relative to Biblical standards and her future as a nation.

Various recent polls indicate between 60% and 70% of Americans believe that this great nation is headed in the wrong direction. Reasons for this dissatisfaction include the nearly stagnant economy, the high unemployment rate, and our failed mid-east foreign policy.

Very seldom do citizens suggest that we are headed in the wrong direction due to our abandonment of Biblical principles. Many subscribe to the premise that inasmuch as God is love, this nation is in good hands and all will turn out well. Such thinking lines the road to disaster.

Yes, the Bible does state that God is love, but He is also just, holy, righteous, immutable, and sovereign. He is sovereign because He created man in His image and has planned the ultimate outcome for mankind and planet earth from the beginning.

Sadly, according to the Bible, man is constantly getting in the way by side-stepping God's instructions and replacing them with his own agenda. That strategy will certainly result in failure.

There comes a point when God will withdraw His hand of protection and turn men loose to pursue their own way. That defines the 'point of no return.'

There are numerous scripture references addressing this issue.

"Because I have called and you refused, I have stretched out my hand and no one regarded, because you disdained all my counsel, and would have none of my rebuke, I also will laugh at your calamity; I will mock when your terror comes...when distress and anguish come upon you. Then they will call on me, but I will not answer; they will seek me diligently, but they will not find me. Because they hated knowledge and did not choose the fear of the LORD, they would have none of my counsel... therefore they shall eat the fruit of their own way, and be filled to the full with their own fancies." Proverbs 1:24-31 NKJV

Several issues are highlighted in this scripture.

- God will have revealed Himself to all mankind.
- The majority have refused God's counsel.
- There comes a point where God removes His hand of protection.
- Man will indeed reap what he has sown.

There are numerous times in the Old Testament where references to Israel could accurately be applied to America.

"But My people did not listen to My voice; and Israel did not obey Me. So I gave them over to the stubbornness of their heart, to walk in their own devices (counsels). Oh that My people would listen to Me, that Israel would walk in My ways! I would quickly subdue their enemies, and turn My hand against their adversaries." Psalms 81:11-14 NASB

There comes a time when a non-repentant nation will be told to depend on their self-made gods in time of trouble.

"So the LORD said to the children of Israel, 'Did I not deliver you from the Egyptians and from the Amorites...Yet you have forsaken Me and served other gods. Therefore I will deliver you no more. Go and cry out to the gods which you have chosen; let them deliver you in your time of distress.'" Judges 10:11-14 NKJV

"...the LORD is with you when you are with Him. And if you seek Him, He will let you find Him; but if you forsake Him, He will forsake you." 2 Chronicles 15:2b NASB

The Bible also compares the world's wisdom with God's wisdom.

"The wicked, in the haughtiness (pride) of his countenance, does not seek Him. All his thoughts are, 'There is no God.'" Psalms 10:4 NASB

"There is a way which seems right to a man, but its end is the way of death." Proverbs 14:12 NASB

The point of no return for a nation is reached when that nation continually ignores God with no intention of changing their ways.

"And you shall speak all these words to them, but they will not listen to you; and you shall call to them, but they will not answer you." Jeremiah 7:27 NASB

At that point God says not to even pray for that nation. Their judgment cannot be averted.

"Therefore do not pray for this people, nor lift up a cry or prayer for them nor make intercession to Me; for I will not hear you." Jeremiah 7:16 NKJV

The solution for our nation's woes is quite straightforward.

"Thus says the LORD of hosts... 'Obey My voice, and I will be your God, and you shall be My people. And walk in all the ways that I have commanded you that it may be well with you.'" Jeremiah 7:21-23 NKJV

And let us not forget President Obama's infamous and naïve statement made in his 'new beginning' speech in Cairo in 2009. His purpose was to unite the varied cultures and religions of the world.

"We have the power to make the world we seek…the people of the world can live together in peace. We know this is God's vision."

America is technically a constitutional republic which is in broader terms, a democracy. A democracy is based on the premise that the majority rules.

And remember, in all nations the majority are void of kingdom wisdom.

Has America as a nation passed the point of no return?

Printed in the United States
By Bookmasters